PRAISE FOR STEALING BABY JESUS

With *Stealing Baby Jesus,* memoirist and gifted storyteller Bernadette Nason sits us down for another round of cozy tales. Here, she plays the Spirit of Christmas Past, revisiting memories, adventures, and misadventures from her life—her childhood in England, her expat years working in Tripoli and Dubai, and even her three decades as, heaven help her, a Brit among Texans—all related to the yuletide. Each episode opens with a quote from *A Christmas Carol,* but Nason has taken more from that well-known work than Dickens' words; she's absorbed its lesson that the heart of the holiday lies in generosity and warmth and good cheer, for her stories are as full of them as one of the Fezziwigs' holiday parties.

—**Robert Faires,** *Austin Chronicle*

Merry Christmas to us all! Bernadette Nason's *Stealing Baby Jesus* is a gift—a globe-trotting, holiday-saving adventure through time—given to us with all the heart, candor, humor, hopefulness, and modest worry one could ask of a self-respecting English person. Weaving Dickens' *A Christmas Carol* through as the common thread, or ribbon if you will, Nason gently offers her true holiday tales—dreamy wishes not quite met, difficult events turned triumphant, the howling emptiness of a missing person from the holiday table, the indescribable rush of theatrical success—all with the knowing hand and soothing nature of the best of storytellers. Her plucky perseverance is contagious, and this collection of Christmas stories is a welcome reminder that good people still try (and sometimes succeed) to make things magical.

—**Beth Burns,** *Artistic Director, The Hidden Room Theatre*

To read *Stealing Baby Jesus* is like sitting in a coffee shop with Bernadette Nason and sharing Christmas stories that remain as vivid as the day they happened. This book comes to the reader as a movie, highly visual, active and colorful. Nason writes with such transparency and authenticity that the reader finds it effortless to go along on her hugely varied and emotional memory trips, even though they span continents and decades. While this story is wholly her own, it will surely conjure readers' memories as well as inspire some honest retrospection. *Stealing Baby Jesus* is at once a fun and thoughtful read.

—**Joy H. Selak, PhD**, *Chartered Advisor in Philanthropy and Author of CeeGee's Gift*

Bernadette Nason's high-adrenaline tales of Christmases past teeter on the edge of heartbreak and hilarity as she chases holiday cheer in the unlikeliest of places across the globe, from a bitterly cold December in Thatcher-era England to a Dubai desert paradise and finally to Texas. Under Nason's endearing comic spell, Christmas may not always be the most wonderful time of the year, but it never fails to be unforgettable.

—**Sarah Chandler**, *Lonely Planet author, and Writing Studies faculty at the University of Minnesota, Twin Cities*

Bernadette Nason's *Stealing Baby Jesus* is a joyous follow up to her adventurous first memoir, *Tea in Tripoli*. Her delightfully wry sense of humor shines through on every heartwarming page. Nason takes us on a nostalgic journey that will make you laugh out loud, wipe a tear from your eye and put a glow in your heart.

—**Lynn S. Beaver**, *BroadwayWorld Austin*

Nason has a magical way of expressing herself in writing—maybe it's the storyteller in her that makes every anecdote feel so alive.

—**Anne Glasgow**, *Supporter of the Arts and Lifetime Reader*

Bernadette Nason

STEALING
BABY JESUS

**A Treasury of Ludicrous Attempts
to Rescue Christmas**

Brave Bear & Company
2900 West Anderson Lane, C200/302
Austin, TX 78757
Copyright © 2020 by Bernadette Nason

This memoir is a work of creative nonfiction. Events, locales and conversations have been recreated to the best of the author's memory. If the
author could not recall the exact words said by certain people, and exact
descriptions of certain things, she has filled in gaps as best she could.
Otherwise, all characters, incidents and dialogue are real, and are not
products of the author's imagination. While all the stories in this book are
true, names and some identifying details have been changed to protect
the privacy of the people involved.

Every effort has been made to trace copyright holders and to obtain their
permission for the use of copyright material. The author apologizes for
any errors or omissions in the above list and would be grateful if notified
of any corrections that should be incorporated in future reprints or edi-
tions of this book.

The author may be available to attend live events. For details, please visit
bernadettenason.com.

Library of Congress Cataloging-in-Publication Data
Nason, Bernadette
Stealing Baby Jesus: A Treasury of Ludicrous Attempts to Rescue Christ-
mas / Bernadette Nason

1. Christmas—Memories 2. Memoir—Humor—Nason
3. Holidays—Personal Stories

PN 6071 N53 2020   818.92 Na

ISBN Paperback: 978-0-9987848-2-3
ISBN Digital: 978-0-9987848-3-0

Cover design by Trevor Lemoine

Printed in the USA
2 3 4 5 6 7 8 9 10

STEALING BABY JESUS

To my mother, Elizabeth Ashlin-Wood

For my family and friends who lived these adventures with me

And everyone who celebrates Christmas every day

ACKNOWLEDGEMENTS

Sincere appreciation to my fabulous readers (Anne Glasgow, Donna Ingham, Buffy, Ian, and Christie Manners), and to Danielle Acee, Sally Grenard-Moore, Sara Kocek, Kathryn Rogers, and the Writers' League of Texas. To Trevor Lemoine for his sterling work on the cover, always running with my ideas and injecting them with his own brilliance. To every member of the Ingham and Manners' families for being my Austin Christmas and Boxing Day support for over a decade. To Anne Hulsman, Michael Stuart, Lara Toner Haddock and Don Toner and my theatre family at Austin Playhouse. Love and gratitude to my own English family for sharing all those Christmases with me. To Beckwith and Eli Payne for accepting a wicked stepmother into their lives. And special love and praise to John Payne for listening to these tales, mostly without complaint, for over twenty-five years, reading several drafts, constantly cheering me on, and accepting my annual seasonal experiments. Here's to Christmases yet to come!

CONTENTS

FOREWORD

I had read Charles Dickens' *A Christmas Carol*, my favorite book, every December since I was a teenager, and acted in productions of it for twenty years. By 2015, I was so friggin' bored with it, I decided to drop it for a year. Instead, I would choose four real-life anecdotes from my own Christmases past—one from each country I'd lived in—and perform them at Hyde Park Theatre as a one-woman show entitled *Stealing Baby Jesus*. My friends were super supportive, and my longtime theatrical accomplice, Michael Stuart, agreed to direct my efforts. ScriptWorks generously awarded me a small grant with which to pay him. Michael is a great actor/director; what he doesn't know about theatre isn't worth knowing. I especially enjoy our collaborations because he tells me when my work is crap. Nicely, of course, but no holds barred. And he's witty: he spots humor where I've missed it. Also, he'll work at my house when rehearsal space is not available, which is always.

Stealing Baby Jesus would be difficult to pull off, especially in December, when everyone is busy, but I could do it, I knew I could; I'd done solo shows before. What I didn't foresee, even bearing in mind that Michael didn't have a car or a working computer or a printer, was just how difficult it would be to do every single element of the production myself, at the same time as editing the script, learning the lines, and rehearsing the play. What about marketing? How about actually getting butts in seats?

Poster design: Trevor Lemoine

On the day of opening, I remember delivering programs (designed, executed, printed, folded, and paid for by me) to the theatre, then racing home to shower and collect my make-up and costume (a new one from Target because the original outfit hadn't worked with the lighting), before driving straight back to the theatre to get ready, all the time running lines, many of them newly written, in my head, and aloud wherever possible.

In the dressing room before I went on, I prayed some friends would join me for opening. Such nights are important to actors, all the more so when you're the only one performing. Only ten people had booked, which certainly wouldn't help pay for the theatre; most of them were comps, anyway. Perhaps I'd get walk-ups, I thought. I prayed for walk-ups. More than the money, I needed the energy of a live audience to carry me through this performance. How could I carry it if there was no one to respond, no one to love and appreciate my work? I'd be fine as long as I could absorb some of that glorious crowd energy.

2

At 8:00 p.m., the lights went up and I made my entrance. I took a breath and looked into the "crowd." There were seven people; five in the front row (fully lit so I could see their faces) and two in the back row (out of sight). The five consisted of John (ex-husband current boyfriend), Anne Hulsman (dear friend, fresh from running the box office), Shanon Weaver (reviewer), Michael Meigs (reviewer) and his wife, Karen. In the back row was another reviewer and his girlfriend. Three reviewers.

A good review would certainly have helped with marketing, but to get a good review, I'd need to do a fabulous performance, wouldn't I? Well, I didn't. I gave one of sorriest performances of my career to date. I didn't mean to. What usually happens with this storyteller/actress is that adrenaline floods my system the moment I open my mouth and words begin to flow. I had nothing. I could hardly recall what I was doing there. I could not rise above the sight of that almost empty theatre. I was enervated by sadness, weak with worthlessness. All my work, all the hours and days and weeks of rehearsing, all those months of writing. I was witnessing myself bomb. I somehow managed to get the thing moving, like a half-dead dinosaur, muscle memory kicking in at last, but my strength ebbed and flowed. A few times, I had to stop myself from holding up my hands in defeat and saying, "Why don't we cut our losses, and go home? Pretend this never happened."

That night was, quite honestly, one of the worst nights of my stage career, if that's what we'd call my theatre life in Austin. It's high on my list of worst nights ever, but perhaps that's over-dramatic. I'm an actress, after all. I will say this. When it was over, I thought my acting career was over, too.

The two front-row critics were kind and didn't review the show, bless them. The third one did, and it wasn't good. He could see there were possibilities and hoped I'd rise to the occasion in future performances.

All was not lost, though. *(Cue music: What a difference a day makes...)* The following night yielded a different show: full of vivacity and vision, and also full of people who responded and—if appearances didn't deceive—who loved and appreciated my work.

3

Sob! Another reviewer came along and penned a glowing appraisal, documenting the joy I'd bestowed, and how she hoped *Stealing Baby Jesus* might become a modern tradition. Even more noteworthy is that audiences waited after the performances to chat about Christmas, about family traditions and about their own experiences, good and bad. On closing night, I was honored by a standing ovation and resounding cheers. All had not been lost.

When it was done and dusted, a few people cc'ed me on articles they'd been inspired to write about the changing concept of the Holiday season. I also got messages requesting "more Christmas disaster stories," which eventually encouraged me to compile this treasury.

As I mention in my memoir *Tea in Tripoli*, I've tried to ensure the accuracy of historical facts, but I can't vouch for my memories. As a professional storyteller and writer, I recognize that it's possible for the same story to be told in many distinctive ways. Indeed, that's one of the joys of the art. It's the same with personal narratives. My siblings and I can't agree on the precise details of anything. Think of your own family. Point of view is everything.

Thus, with apologies to those who shared these experiences if my recollection doesn't match theirs, these are my memories and, for better or worse, this is my story.

Bernadette Nason
Austin, Texas
August 2020

PS My husband, John, and I were married in 1994, divorced in 2010, and consciously re-coupled in 2013. We're been together ever since. Although this makes sense as the book progresses, I write it now so as to avoid confusion.

PPS I have changed some names, and my brother actively dislikes my writing about him, so he becomes simply Big Bro or Bro. Although my sister is fine with it, I've kept mention of her name to a minimum. My mother, on the other hand, not only loved sharing her writing with me, she loved to be included in *my* writing, so she's all over this book. In many ways, she's the star of the show. I'm happy to take the supporting role.

"I have endeavoured in this Ghostly little book, to raise the Ghost of an Idea, which shall not put my readers out of humour with themselves, with each other, with the season, or with me. May it haunt their houses pleasantly, and no one wish to lay it.

Their faithful Friend and Servant,

C. D. "

A NOTE FROM THE AUTHOR

This little book has been written as an entertainment. It is not intended to teach or preach or convince you of anything. It's not about religion. I'm not trying to convert you and I don't need to be converted. It's my attempt to share—with humor, with compassion for both myself and others, perhaps even with a little insight into the human condition—how I have worked and continue to work through my issues with Christmas and everything connected with it.

It would be easy to advise me that having deeper faith in God and Jesus and the Christmas story could be the answer to my dilemmas, but it isn't that simple. Nothing is ever that simple. I'm not looking for advice. Please don't offer any. If you read this little book for any reason other than an opportunity to laugh and cry and visit people with different customs in other parts of the world, you may be disappointed. But if you pick it up with an open heart and mind, I reckon you'll be entertained. It's also possible you'll find yourself considering yuletide customs in your family home, and laughing hysterically at some of your Christmases past, or maybe even asking a question or two about your own seasonal sadness. Who knows?

For my part, I write only to divert and amuse and lift your spirits. With that in mind. . . .

CHAPTER 1

Introduction
"The Most Wonderful Time of the Year!"

"Merry Christmas?! Out upon Merry Christmas! If I could work my will," said Scrooge indignantly, *"every idiot who goes about with 'Merry Christmas' on his lips should be boiled with his own pudding, and buried with a stake of holly through his heart!"*

Every time I hear Andy Williams sing "It's the most wonderful time of the year…" I want to reach out, grab the nearest person, and punch that person in the face. Naturally, I would try to smile while doing so—it is Christmas, after all. That song, written specifically for Andy Williams by Eddie Pola and George Wyle (the latter of whom also wrote the theme song to *Gilligan's Island* so he's got a lot to answer for), was a hit in 1963, about the time my own Christmas story begins.

Frankly, I've always dreaded December. With a multitude of gloomy Holiday memories, from childhood to this day, I've been known to say that I hate Christmas, particularly when I've got a martini under my belt. It's not true. Don't believe a word of it. I've been drinking. I don't hate it. I struggle with it. And, to be honest, I'm obsessed with it, too. I could title this book: "My Obsession with the Season and My Annual Disappointment at How It Turns Out."

My earliest memory of Christmas Day—I'm four; my sister is three; and my brother, six—is of spending it with my parents at the house of Dad's "lady-friend," Hazel. I can't claim to recollect much about it, but I do recall wondering why we weren't spending it at home where our "big presents" had been laid out ready for us to open and where Father Christmas had already filled our stockings with little gifts, along with the baffling oranges and mixed nuts in their shells (such odd things to give a child). And, in spite of my age, I did get a feeling that the atmosphere was strange, that Mum and Dad didn't have much to say to each other . . . not that they ever did, come to think of it. The grown-ups were extremely polite and controlled, and we kids seemed to know instinctively that we should be the same, in spite of Christmas Day being the day of all days we most eagerly anticipated, a day that should, by rights, be *un*controlled and riotous.

I'm guessing, because I was too young to know for sure, that my family's yuletide eccentricity started right there in "Auntie Hazel's" front room, with its artificial tree and good behavior. I can't tell you exactly when our father did a bunk with a different lady, whom we knew as "Auntie Betty," but it was probably before the following Christmas because our stacks of handwritten letters to him start around that time.

This, then, would be when my reserved, stouthearted, for-all-practical-purposes-single mother commenced her admirable efforts to "create Christmas" for her children, developing a long list of cheap (free) activities to keep us entertained throughout December, when we most missed our father, when his absence seemed almost unbearable.

In retrospect, Mum's "things to do" were pretty impressive, bearing in mind she had to pull it off alone in a southern English city where she knew hardly a soul, while taking care of three desolate children. There wasn't a proliferation of DIY craft books in 1960s Britain, at least not for a woman with no money, and other than her trips to the library, she didn't have easy access to reading matter; there was no internet. If her "create Christmas" activities were remarkable—and I believe they were—then my personal attempts to follow her traditions in adult life are remarkable, too, just in a different way (not blowing my trumpet here, as you'll appreciate in the chapters to come). It's also fair to say that my endeavors at building my own traditions have been equally challenging, often bringing about the same annual Boxing Day questions: "Where did I go wrong? What can I do differently next year? Who wants a drink?"

I invite you, then, to travel the world with me, and experience surprising and frequently absurd Christmas adventures in England, Africa, Arabia, and America, as I undertake to restore a positive, lighthearted attitude to the Holidays, investigating my pessimism, and discovering that there's a lot more to 25th December than holly, mistletoe, and sherry.

CHAPTER 2

Christmas with the Family
a.k.a. The Big Freeze

"It was cold, bleak, biting weather: foggy withal: and (Ebenezer Scrooge) could hear the people in the court outside, go wheezing up and down, beating their hands upon their breasts, and stamping their feet upon the pavement stones to warm them."

I was three years old as England transitioned from the traumatized 1950s into the strange new world that was the Sixties. World War II had ended in 1945 and rationing in England in 1954, but their repercussions continued for years. Postwar Britain sincerely believed it was possible to restore the status quo, and the average Englishman thought life would get back to normal. However, both Britannia and Joe Public had another think coming. The status quo had changed. There was a new "normal" in town, and "normal," as they knew it, would never exist again.

In those times, at least in my day-to-day world, people maintained the old ways. Most folk "lived on the never-never" which meant putting down a deposit on something you needed, like a washing machine or fridge, then paying for it over a period of time because that was the only way you could afford it— a bit like using a credit card, except you didn't get what you wanted until it was paid for. People typically lived close to work and could walk there. Couples clung to unhappy marriages, because no one got divorced back then. As a Catholic, I believed divorce was actually impossible. Did all this grown-up stuff resonate with me? Not really. I'd hear my mother refer to "postwar England" and have no idea what she meant by it. Children were generally unaware of parental issues, living almost separate lives, being kept in the dark about serious events. Adults often said "Not in front of the children," unconscious of how puzzling and challenging it is for kids not to know what's going on at home. Therapists probably earn most of their money helping us deal with family secrets.

There was a simplicity about an English Christmas in the early 1960s. From conversations with my peers, it seems our seasonal celebrations were so similar, we might as well have been in the same house, the only difference being that, if you were Catholic, you had to go to church. Otherwise, everyone had an Advent calendar (though most non-Catholics may not have known what Advent was), a decorated tree, and stockings from Father Christmas (with stupid oranges and nuts). Everyone experienced frenzied gift-opening of "big" presents from family members and out-of-town relatives. Gifts were a lot more modest then and usually didn't cost much: "it's the thought that counts" was the maxim of the day. What this really meant was that you had to try to show appreciation for whatever you'd been given, even if it was a piece of crap.

A grand turkey and stuffing dinner (with roast potatoes, Brussels sprouts, garden peas, brown gravy, and sometimes Yorkshire pudding and even a ham), followed by plum pudding and custard or cream or brandy butter for dessert, was served in the afternoon to accommodate the Queen's speech on the radio (or the black-and-white telly) at or around 3:00 p.m. Before we chowed down, we'd pull crackers,* share the mottoes and jokes, acknowledge the tiny trashy plastic toys, and put on the flimsy colored paper hats for the rest of the day. (From the youngest age, Sis hated those hats: "We all look so *silly!*" she'd claim.) The massive dinner was *immediately* followed by a pot of tea, Christmas cake, and mince pies with cream, after which everyone passed out or vomited from overindulgence. In the evening, if they weren't still trying to swallow down their tea, folks ate cold turkey and ham sandwiches with Haywards Pickled Onions, Branston Pickle, and

Colman's Mustard. They re-assessed presents, and children played with theirs; sometimes, if folks weren't comatose, party games took place. In later years, English families took to watching the TV on which there might be a Christmas movie, a variety show, or the annual pantomime* at the London Palladium Theatre.

If I bury the blurry memory of "Auntie Hazel," the first Christmas I consciously remember is that of 1962, when I was five, the year the Beatles burst on the scene with *Love Me Do*, James Bond began spying on celluloid in *Dr. No*, and Golden Wonder introduced cheese & onion crisps.

It was snowing heavily on the day Jesus was born; we all learned that from the pictures on Christmas cards. Consequently, British children prayed every year for a white Christmas, and Catholic children like me prayed specifically to the Baby Jesus. That year, the Baby Jesus, bless his cotton socks, stepped up to the plate and knocked it out of the park. The Miracle Baby delivered what is now called "The Big Freeze," the worst UK winter since the 1700s.

It had already snowed in mid-December, so children country-wide were hopeful that a white Christmas might be literally heading our way. It didn't actually snow on the Day itself—terribly disappointing. However, it was bitterly cold, and walking to St. Peter's Roman Catholic Church for morning mass was cold and frosty enough to keep us happy.

I remember that particular Christmas with pleasure—mostly. My parents (Dad was home) were inspired to give my sister and me giant teddy bears as our big presents, teddies almost as big as we were. Sis immediately named hers Martin Christopher Robert James. Mine was Jane Victoria Barbara Edith. . . don't ask, no idea. We carried them around with us all day, so pleased were we with these new friends. They remained our companions for years; Janie lives with me to this day.

The first real snow fell the day after Christmas. It may be different now, but in my youth, Boxing Day, as it's called in England, was when adults recovered from festive over indulgence and tried to decipher the thank-you lists written during the present-opening riots. Children revisited new acquisitions: toys, books, games, fluffy animals, and STUFF. They started jigsaws, built Lego towers, lounged on the sofa with *The Guinness Book of Records*. Everyone contentedly ate leftovers, unaware that they'd be eating that same food for weeks or, in the case of the cake, months to come. In some ways, Boxing Day still felt like Christmas to us; every effort was made to extend the celebrations of the day before.

My siblings and I were experiencing our first real snow. We knew as soon as we awoke that something was up; the light is quite different after a snowfall. And when we ran to our bedroom windows and saw for ourselves, we screamed with delight. "For crying out loud!" my mother whispered loudly from the second-floor landing, "Keep the noise down; we don't want to wake Daddy. And someone let the flippin' cat in! I can hear her from the bathroom!" Smokey the Cantankerous was always forced to go out at night; otherwise, she woke us up with continuous whining and howling. I ran down and opened the back door and, without having realized the severity of the weather, shrieked with glee at the sight of the winter wonderland. The snow was easily a foot deep, and there was Smokey, concertinaed up against the wall of the house, trying to maintain dignity while staying dry. Grumpy at the best of times, this neglect gave reason to her misery and fueled her crabbiness until springtime.

Mum told us that, when she was a child, she'd had a brilliant sledge that got constant use because of the severity of winters in the north of England, where she grew up. She waxed lyrical about that sledge, adding somewhat bitterly that her stepmother had forbidden her to take it away with her when she was last there so it remained at the old vicarage in Gateshead, County Durham, where her father was vicar. Our own father had promised to make us a sledge, but each winter he spent more and more time away from home and, although the bones of it had been prepared, he'd never finished it. Now that opportunity had arisen, what else could we use? Surely there was an alternative.

Sis and me in the snow

Rummaging through the house, we found nothing. Then Mum suggested the old tin tray that she occasionally used for serving afternoon tea. We called it "the old tin tray," but was it tin? I've no clue: silver-colored metal, heavily scratched, about 18 inches in diameter, with a sloped 2-inch rim around it. It was definitely old and already looked as if had been used as a giant pie dish, a shower pan, and the wheel of an armored tank. We ourselves had used it as a cricket bat, a medieval shield, and a head-whacking weapon. Desperate as we were, we accepted Mum's offer and made our way to the Arbour, a community park less than five minutes' walk from our house. We took the homemade sled with us, too, because, although it wasn't ready, we felt very Jingle Bells-y, dragging it behind us through the snow. We had to climb a load of steps to the lane leading to the Arbour and were puffing and panting by the time we reached our destination, but it was worth it. The whole area was covered with pristine snow, unsullied but for a few footprints. At the far side of the park was a long sloping bank, which would clearly make an ideal sledding slope. There were trees along the top, and a pathway along the bottom, leading from one side of the park to the other. The path had a few benches alongside, but we wouldn't have to worry about them because there was no way that a sledge or an old tin tray would make it that far. When we got there, only a few other kids had thought of this snow game, and we felt suitably proud that it was pretty much our idea. In fact, children (and adventurous adults) had been using the Arbour bank for winter sports for centuries, but we were too young to know that.

Brother had the first "go" on everything, of course, and Sis wasn't sure she wanted to try at all. Dad's unfinished wooden sled was useless: there was no metal coating on the runners so its luge-like qualities were restricted—i.e., it barely slid on the fresh new snow and would only shift properly when on solid ice, of which there was little to be found. Also, one runner was about half an inch deeper than the other, so that, even when it did move, it would only go straight for a very short distance before turning sideways and passing in front of other people's sleds. Other people weren't happy about this. Other people had toboggans like Olympic bob-sleighs, all shiny metal with minimal wood, and didn't want silly children slowly sliding in front of them when they were going for world records and gold medals.

Bro had just turned eight, and he was a competitor. He wasn't about to be outdone by a bunch of bigger boys with better toys. Dumping the wooden folly at the top of the bank, he grabbed the tin tray. With a running jump onto his makeshift bobsleigh, he shot off the top of the bank as if he'd been catapulted, bounced on the bankside like a downhill skier in mid-run, and whooshed to the bottom at breakneck speed, making it almost as far as the benches. What he hadn't expected, what none of us could've fore-seen, innocent as we were in such winter diversions, was that the tray would spin at the same time as it travelled downhill. There he was, knees up to his ears, arms wrapped around his legs, crouched on Mum's tea tray, spinning like an overactive lazy Susan, his school scarf whipping about him like the arms of a whirling dervish. Having now seen what was possible, both Sis and I wanted a turn. Bro wasn't about to give up his newfound skill, but he eventually showed fra-ternal love and gave us our go. Sis was small and slight, so she didn't go very fast and there wasn't much spinning at all. As middle child, my trip was somewhere in-between: I spun just enough to lose my balance near the bottom and roll off, laughing with ecstatic abandon, into the powdery white. It was pretty much the most fun I'd ever had in my young life. We three were soaked to the skin, freezing cold, and completely exhausted by the time it got dark at 4 p.m., but that was exactly right on a snowy Boxing Day afternoon.

Was Dad still at home when we returned that afternoon, or had he already flown the coop? I couldn't tell you. However, unbeknownst to me or my siblings at the time, our glorious sporting activity seems to have coincided with our father's permanent departure from the family unit, abandoning mother and children, and his swift transition into deadbeat dad, setting up the soon-to-be-annual dilemma: "Will he be home for Christmas?"

CHAPTER 3

December DIY

"But now a knocking at the door was heard, and such a rush imme-diately ensued that she with laughing face and plundered dress was borne towards it the centre of a flushed and boisterous group, just in time to greet the father, who came home attended by a man laden with Christmas toys and presents."

A nd so began our mum's stalwart efforts to "create Christmas" on her own, cultivating a series of low-cost traditions to keep her children's spirits high. . . the virgin birth of Christmas rituals that were to become a part of my life and remain so to this day.

Since my brother's birthday was on 12th December, Christmas events didn't happen much before that date, unless there was a religious or practical reason. Also, in those days, people didn't commence the season as early as they do now. In the UK, we don't celebrate Thanksgiving, so there was no concept of starting the festive fracas until December. Here are the customs leading up to the Big Day, both old and newly created by Mum, as they happened in our house:

- opening the Advent calendar ("Please may we have one with glitter, PLEASE!");
- taking bad-tempered walks in nature to collect holly, leaves, berries, fir-cones, and acorns, to make ornaments for the tree;
- assembling the Nativity;

- baking the Christmas cake;
- attending the Mayor's Christmas Carol Concert;
- celebrating my brother's birthday;
- decorating the Christmas tree;
- taking economy train trips to big cities for seasonal street lights and decorated shop windows;
- visiting budget, shoddy in-store Santas;
- going to school Christmas pageants and/or the pantomime at local theatres;
- singing carols at St. Peter's Church (particularly during primary school years);
- singing carols at Winchester Cathedral (particularly when we were older);
- singing carols in the neighborhood (no one wanted to go, not even for charity);
- giving to charity
- buying or making, then wrapping our own presents and setting them out on Christmas Eve;
- opening stockings on Christmas Day, genuinely believing they come from Father Christmas;
- lighting coal fires in the living room *and* the front room to make the house cheery;
- enjoying a drinks table with specialities: dates, nuts, tangerines, bananas, apple cider for us (non-alcoholic), Dubonnet and sherry for Mum (alcoholic)

A year or two before she died, at my request, Mum recorded reminiscences of family events. Her memory had already begun to fade, and we regularly recalled things differently. However, here's what she wrote about Christmas:

"When the children were very young, there were several things which were done year after year as 'treats.' The first one would be the making of the cake. I would get the old Hoovermatic washing machine out into the middle of the kitchen and sit the children round it on high stools. Then out came the ingredients and the various utensils and we

would start. All the weighing was done taking turns to get it exactly right; then we would start to put everything into the mixing bowl. As the more edible items were reached they would all get a taste: a few currants, sultanas, raisins, one cherry each. No one like candied peel. As the mixture was formed everyone had to do some stirring until it was ready to go into the cake tin. Everyone put some in until only a little of the mix was left. Then there would be cries of "Leave some for us!" and finally as I put the cake into the oven, spoons would be given out and the bowl attacked until it didn't need washing, so thorough was the clearing.

The first of the outings was to see the lights and shops of Southampton. We would go down by train on a Sunday afternoon. No shops were open (on Sundays) in those days of course so it was a cheap outing. We started at the Bargate where there was a big shop called Mays. We spent ages there looking in the windows. There was always a moving display involving Santa and polar bears, or the Sleeping Beauty. Then the toy display was examined, and then on to the next. There were enough department stores to make it quite an event. Behind Above Bar, there was a children's play park and we always went there for a swing and see-saw and slide. I remember how cold it often was and how I wished the wind wasn't blowing up my skirt. We generally found a teashop and had a bun or scone and a drink and then back to the station.

The next outing was in our own city of Winchester when we did the same as in Southampton even including the swing and the slide. This didn't take quite so long because we had no train journey and Winchester is nothing like so big. Even so everything was examined minutely and we particularly looked at the shop where we would be going to see Father Christmas.

This was the next thing. It had to be on a week-day when the shops were open. Nearly always we went to Sheriff and Ward but there were other "grottoes." Once we went to Curry's and it was the worst. Every child received a pair of plastic binoculars regardless of age and sex. Father Christmas was not very polite to me I must say. Still what could you expect for a shilling? On very rare occasions we actually went to Southampton on a weekday and visited one of their grottoes. They were much superior to those on offer at Winchester.

That really took care of the outings. The other events were indoors. I think making cards and perhaps a present came next with about a ton of glitter and a vat of glue. It is impossible to describe the mess. Every family will know it. Each worked according to their age. My son was two years older than Bernie so was properly scornful of anything she had made or decorated. My youngest girl swam in a sea of paper and sticky scissors. Things did get made and were as good as anything any other child did, I'm sure.

Then came the present wrapping done with great secrecy and cries of "You're looking!" It's a wonder anyone received anything at all considering the loss of temper over this important area of preparation. The trouble with the wrapping paper was its thinness. The expensive paper was thicker but we were always watching the pennies so had to make do. Soon little thumbs would poke through, the present itself would show only too clearly exactly what it was and the wrapping paper would end up on the floor, flung down by furious hands. Selotape (Scotchtape) was a disaster, sticky paper which had to be licked was even worse.

This happened in the early days before school took over most of the "art work" but we went on with the outings for many years until my son was too old for such "baby stuff" and only the girls still enjoyed them.

Still, all in all, I remember these days up to Christmas as very rewarding. I wonder if my children think so too."

When I found this piece years later, I cried, struck not only by the similarity of our memories, but also (as has been pointed out to me several times) by our matching writing styles. Then I registered what I hadn't known: her taking us to the park in freezing weather, wearing a skirt (she never wore trousers back then; it wasn't done) that wasn't warm enough, all to provide the best, most enjoyable experience possible. Mum didn't consider herself a maternal woman—and frankly, she wasn't, not in the conventional sense—but it's touching to note how far she was prepared to go to bring us happiness.

*See Appendices

Edwin Jones, Southampton Department Store, 1960s
Photo credit: Daily Echo

CHAPTER 4

Stealing Baby Jesus

"As good as gold," said Bob, "and better. Somehow (Tiny Tim) gets thoughtful sitting by himself so much, and thinks the strangest things you ever heard. He told me, coming home, that he hoped the people saw him in the church, because he was a cripple, and it might be pleasant to them to remember upon Christmas Day, who made lame beggars walk and blind men see."

T he setting up of the crèche in early December each year was a really big deal. We didn't call it a crèche in our house; we called it the crib scene or nativity. Every year, we'd lovingly unpack each item and place it in the open wooden shed: Mary, Joseph, the Baby Jesus, the manger, the angels, the shepherds, the wise men, the sheep, the camels, the donkey, cows, dogs, cats, chickens. As you know, everyone was present at the birth of Jesus on 25th December 0000.

When I was about nine years old, I set out the wooden shed and unwrapped the Nativity pieces, ready to put together the Christmas scene. The previous year, we were devastated when we couldn't find the little manger. I say "we," though I doubt anyone cared as much as I did. We'd had to use an empty matchbox, you know, one of those little purple boxes made of balsa wood. The Baby Jesus nestled in cotton wool quite comfortably until Epiphany on 6th January. But this year I was horrified to discover that the Baby Jesus had disappeared, too. I scrabbled desperately through the nativity tin, but it wasn't there. The cardboard boxes of decorations were stored in a dark and spooky area known as "the little room under the stairs" where murderers could hide (or worse, spiders) so Mum had to do the initial schlepping. We'd enjoy unwrapping them, oohing and aahing over each piece, but when it was all over, she'd have to pack them up. I can imagine myself accusing her: "Mummy, you must've dropped the Baby Jesus last year!" And I can hear her declaring: "You kids like the fun part, but I always have to clear everything away!" *It was almost certainly her fault*, I'd have judged, needing to lay blame; *You owe me, Mother!* Whoever was responsible, now we had no Baby Jesus and no manger. This was serious. I don't mean to sound pitiful, but when I was growing up, there wasn't the kind of ready cash people seem to have nowadays, not in my family anyway, and there certainly weren't any credit cards. The loss of the Baby Jesus *and* his manger was huge.

It so happened that the next Saturday morning I found myself walking around Woolworth's on Winchester High Street. I believe Woolworth's in America was the same as Woolworth's in England: long aisles with shop assistants marching up and down like prison guards, keeping an eye on counters that were filled with goodies, everything costing under a shilling, (less than a quarter). Pretty cheap.

I wasn't looking for a Baby Jesus. I really wasn't. Walking around Woolworth's on a Saturday morning was simply one of my favorite things to do. If nine years old seems young to you for a child to be walking around the streets of a city's downtown area, I can only say that everything was safer then. My mother never worried about me; there was never anything to worry about.

My favorite counter was the sweet counter, displaying an enormously diverse selection of loose candy in clear plastic bins. It was a youngster's delight. If I list the sweets, it's possible that only Brits will have the slightest idea what I'm talking about. Maybe it's the same goodies as in other countries, but with different names. We had flying saucers: rice paper with sherbet in the middle, which you sucked until the rice paper melted, stuck to the roof of your mouth, and shot the sherbet down your throat, choking you half to death. We had shrimps: large, pink, shrimp-shaped lumps of sugary stuff that tasted a bit like bubble gum but had the texture of sweet rubber. You'd chew and chew and chew until your mouth was bright pink, like I imagined it would be if you'd eaten a whole, raw lobster. Never having seen a whole, raw lobster, I knew no better.

Interior of Winchester Woolworth's showing the sweet counter (I think)

And it so happened that right next to the sweet counter was the *little plastic objects counter*. If America these days has a lot of things with "Made in China" written on them, in England in the Sixties, it was "Made in Hong Kong." Every little plastic object was made in Hong Kong. All of a sudden, I had magpie syndrome. My eyes were drawn to all these bright, shiny things, and the one that attracted me most was a brightly colored, very shiny Baby Jesus in a manger. Not just a Baby Jesus, not just a manger, but two-in-one.

I left the sweet counter and went to look close up. There must've been hundreds of Baby Jesuses in the Baby Jesus section, all exactly the same. I didn't care; the more the merrier. Let everyone have a shiny, plastic, made-in-Hong-Kong Baby Jesus in a manger. I wanted only one. I picked up the topmost of these delicate items and held it carefully in my little girl hands. The manger was brown and shiny, the straw was yellow and shiny, the baby Jesus was wrapped in swaddling clothes, white and shiny. The king of kings had an actual face with an actual facial expression. He was lovely and very real. Frankly, he was much nicer than our old Baby Jesus, who was *tiny*, and whose face was so small there was no expression, not even any features to speak of. This was a superb piece of craftsmanship. Really, it was. It didn't matter that there were hundreds of them, all exactly the same. It was, quite honestly, the most beautiful thing I'd ever seen.

I turned it over to look at the price. Sixpence, which was half a shilling, a good bit less than a quarter. So it was cheap. But when you're nine, it has to be really cheap, and it wasn't cheap enough. Would my mum pay for it? I pictured the scene, Mum in the middle of making dinner.

Mummy, you know that we can't find the Baby Jesus.
Yes, dear.
And you know we've lost the manger as well.
I know, dear. It's very sad.
I saw a nice Baby Jesus in a manger at Woolworth's, Mummy. Not just a Baby Jesus but a Baby Jesus in a manger. Will you buy it for us?
Haven't you got any pocket money left, dear?
No, Mum. I spent it on sweets.
Well, I'm sorry, love, but I haven't got any money to spare at the moment.
But Mum, it's only sixpence.
I'm afraid I don't have sixpence. Why don't you make one out of a pine cone, darling? I know you can.
But Mummy...

A pine cone? I didn't think I could. What was she thinking? I mean, she was the one who'd lost the Baby Jesus and probably the manger too. Surely sixpence wasn't too much to ask. I was seething with resentment at our imagined conversation; I could almost feel myself scowling. Well, if she wasn't going to pay for it, what was I going to do? I needed the Baby Jesus in a manger; no, *we* needed the Baby Jesus in a manger. I looked at the splendid object in my hand. That's when I had an idea. A really bad idea.

The guard of the shiny plastic objects counter was Mrs. Ratty, a neighbor with a long, pointed face and beady eyes, who'd always rather frightened me. Mum once said, "How awful to be called Mrs. Ratty when you actually look like a rat." I waited until she reached the end of the counter, and in the split second before she turned around to walk back in my direction, I slipped the beautiful baby into the pocket of my anorak. I stole it! I didn't mean to. It was almost without awareness. My mind had flickered for a tiny moment. And it was *so easy*. Immediately, as fast as I'd pinched it, I wanted to put it back, but Mrs. Ratty turned and looked right at me with her beady eyes. It was too late. The deed was done. I had joined the criminal class. Glancing around to see if anyone had noticed the change in me, I made my way to the exit. Sick to my stomach, I slunk out of the shop.

I had never stolen anything before; you can only imagine my sense of guilt. Imagine then that you're Catholic and you've stolen something; the guilt is like a tangible, living thing. And now imagine that you're Catholic and you've stolen *the Baby Jesus*. The gates of Hell might just as well open up and swallow you, right there and then.

I could see it now. Headlines of the Winchester Catholic Digest: *Nine-year-old Bernadette Nason of Elm Road, Winchester, was arrested today for stealing a shiny, plastic, made-in-Hong-Kong Baby Jesus in a manger from Woolworth's. Peter Paul Bogan, head-master of St. Peter's Roman Catholic School is quoted as saying, "She always seemed like such a nice girl. I suppose the Devil works in mysterious ways too."*

I hardly remember the walk home. The blessed infant burned a hole in my pocket. I tried to justify my actions: it was Mum's fault, not mine; no one would miss one Baby Jesus when there were hundreds of them; I'd be the family hero! Nothing worked. That glittering prize in swaddling clothes was so hot, my hand dripped with the sweat of shame.

When I got home, I took the offending object out of my pocket and hung my anorak on the hall stand. Heart thumping, mouth dry, I stood before the family Nativity and looked at the scene. Despite my horror at what I'd just done, I smiled as I placed the stolen merchandise in the middle of the wooden stall so that Mary and Joseph could once again pick up their roles as mother and foster father (or was it stepfather?) to the Son of God. But there was something I hadn't considered, something that wouldn't have occurred to a child of nine. The shiny, plastic, made-in-Hong-Kong Baby Jesus in a manger was bigger than his parents. The object was massive, at least compared with the Holy Mum and Dad. Our Mary and Joseph were elegant and, well, small. My too-hot-to-handle Holy Babe was gigantic. It was like setting a monster tractor in a room full of Lamborghinis. Mary and Joseph would've required a stepladder just to gaze down on him lovingly. I was just beginning to realize the ridiculousness of the situation when my mother walked into the room.

I didn't enjoy the walk back to Woolworth's. Humble pie with a big dollop of groveling apology was difficult for me to swallow. I hadn't even had time to appreciate the error of my ways before being caught in the act. There were no criminal repercussions, no shame-filled stories repeated at a later date—until now, anyway— and no punishment that I recall. Mum had her own methods of instilling morals. Her quiet disappointment was almost more than a person could stand. A daily glance at the matchbox with cotton wool and an imaginary baby which sufficed that year for the glorious newborn was enough to remind me that stealing Baby Jesus wasn't the way to build a crib, wasn't the way to please my mother, and certainly wasn't the way to get to Heaven.

CHAPTER 5

Hot Cross Nun

"Mr. Scrooge!" said Bob; "I'll give you Mr. Scrooge, the Founder of the Feast!"

"The Founder of the Feast indeed!" cried Mrs. Cratchit, reddening. "I wish I had him here. I'd give him a piece of my mind to feast upon, and I hope he'd have a good appetite for it."

"My dear," said Bob, "the children; Christmas Day."

"It should be Christmas Day, I am sure," said she, "on which one drinks the health of such an odious, stingy, hard, unfeeling man as Mr. Scrooge."

Everyone was afraid of Sister Mary. She was American, and that was quite enough to scare a diffident English child who'd never met an American before, and "Mayen, shay taweckd funny." I have a clear memory of her full black nun's habit with white around the face and a long black veil. Her crucifix hung down in front of her like a weapon, and when she walked—always very fast as if she were genuinely "on a mission from God"—it would swing from side to side ready to smite any child who got in her way. No one from my past has been able to confirm that image, and I do wonder how much I've been influenced by the nuns in *The Sound of Music*. I've a feeling that *The Blues Brothers* may also be involved. When I first saw Sister Mary Stigmata (a.k.a. the Penguin), I just knew on whom the character was based.

When I started school at age four, school lunches were provided for one shilling, about fifteen cents. (Today, as I write, they cost two pounds sterling, about three dollars.) We used to walk from St. Peter's Roman Catholic Primary School* on Gordon Road, across North Walls, along St. Peter's Street to Milner Hall, which was then the Catholic social centre but which had been the original boys' school, when the girls were taught by Benedictine nuns in what is now the hoity-toity Royal Hotel across the street.

In those days, lunches were served from giant metal pots (to me, they were cauldrons) by dinner ladies who said things like, "Eat your cabbage; it'll make your hair curl" or "Don't leave anything on your plate; think of the starving children in Africa." We always said, "I hate curly hair," and "If the African children want it, they can have it!" We complained bitterly about the quality of the food, but looking back, the meals were pretty good: meat, potatoes at least one other vegetable, and always fish on Friday because, as you know, Jesus always had fish on Friday. School puddings were sweet and stodgy delights that I'd scarf down, unless desiccated coconut was glued on top with jam, thereby ruining them. I still hate coconut unless it's in a pina colada.

After a year or two, a new hall and kitchens were added to the school building so we no longer had to walk to lunch. By this time, Sister Mary had joined the school to teach the "first class," or pre-K. I was grateful to have missed her by one year. She lived with the other nuns in the building next door to the presbytery where the priests lived. These two buildings were sandwiched between Milner Hall and St. Peter's Roman Catholic Church. I don't know about "servants of God" or "brides of Christ"; it seemed to me, after doing all the cooking and cleaning, they were more like "charladies to the clergy."

Anyway, the traditional mealtime prayer of thanks was always said before we ate our food: "Bless us, O Lord, and these thy gifts which we are about to receive from thy bounty, through Christ, Our Lord. Amen."

Although the headmaster, Mr. Bogan—Mr. Peter Paul not-just-one-saints-name-but-two Bogan—sometimes said grace, it eventually became Sister Mary's regular job. She'd stand on the steps of the new hall, like a giant white-necked vulture. She'd sign the cross, then: "Bliss us, O Lauwered." She could make "Lord" last for three syllables, i.e., "Bliss us O Lauwered," which I found hilarious and at which I would've snickered, had I not been so completely terrified of her.

Every December, work would begin on the Christmas play, which was usually some sort of nativity. The only time I remember its not being so was when we did *Amahl and the Night Thieves,* which was a thrilling change for our staid Catholic school. In my last year at primary school, when I was ten years old, it was decided to do a different kind of nativity in which none of the children would have to learn lines because there would be a narrator who told the audience everything they needed to know while the kids acted it out alongside. The narrator was the only one who was required to learn anything.

None of this meant anything to me until I was picked to be the narrator. No one had ever asked me to be in a play before! I understand now why I was chosen, but at the time, it came as a surprise. I was frequently teased by schoolmates on account of my standard English accent—perhaps a bit posh compared with the other kids'—so I thought my way of speaking was a negative. Most used the generic "Winchester" accent, a kind-of blend between "West Country" where "oi" is used instead of "I," and a London dialect with its dropped letters: "Oi was 'i'in' (hitting) 'im on the 'ead!" My own accent stemmed from Mum's upper-middle-class upbringing. While she grew up near Newcastle where most people spoke with a Geordie* accent, Mum went to an exclusive boarding school and developed a distinctly plummy voice. Dad had an Irish background, grew up in Gosport on the south coast, and lived in Somerset, so his was a different dialect altogether. However, he wasn't home enough to have much influence on our speech patterns. No matter. I beamed with pride the day I was told, happy to discover my voice was a positive thing, and chuffed to bits to take on the role of narrator. Even at the age of ten I was already considering a career on the stage. I hadn't yet prepared my Oscar acceptance speech—I did that the following year after seeing Barbra Streisand win the award for best lead actress. What a good start this would be!

The only downside of taking on this role was that Sister Mary was to be the director of the show, which meant she'd be at every rehearsal, telling me what to do. Somehow, since the early days of my schooling, I had managed to avoid her ever-more frightening figure as it stormed down the main corridor of our tiny school. As a result of my hiding in doorways and darting about the playground, our paths had never crossed, so the performance in this play was to be my first real encounter with the terrors of Sister Mary.

To my alarm, the narrator had a lot of lines. I don't mean to imply that I grasped, at the impressionable age of ten, how long it would take to *learn* a large number of lines. . . that is not so; I had no idea. However, what I did know and could readily foresee was that there was ample opportunity here for Sister Mary to get on my case and be *displeased* with me. She seemed to be in an almost constant state of displeasure. I was sure that whatever I did, she would be displeased with me. And more than anything in life, I lived in fear of people—anyone at all—being displeased with me. The slightest criticism from any individual except my mother could reduce me to tears in a second, and crying in public was another thing that troubled me. A vicious cycle if ever there was one.

In the early stages of rehearsal, I stood downstage left (that's front left of the stage, for non-theatre folk), reading the lines from the script, as Sister Mary moved the younger children around behind me. The stage wasn't really a stage at all. The hall had two long steps down the length of it, which led to a wide corridor. If you went left along the corridor, you'd come to the front entrance of the school. If you went right, you'd reach the classrooms and eventually the back entrance and playground. Thus, the top step was actually the corridor and became "the stage."

At this point of the proceedings, everything was going quite well. Sister Mary wasn't really taking much notice of me, and I just read my stuff while she rehearsed everyone else. When I wasn't reading, I would stand to the left of the top step, i.e., the stage, facing into the open empty hall (which always smelled of boiled cabbage), and gaze at the pictures on the hall walls. High up on the left of the back wall, there was a large painting of the two fishes and the five loaves. High up on the right, a shield with the crossed keys of St. Peter, after whom the school was named. At the end of the room, on the right-hand wall, taking up most of the width of the room, was a massive colorful mural that I could stare at for hours and always see something new. I'd be lost in contemplation when the nun would suddenly shout in my direction, "Now start reading again!" And off I'd go:

"Christmas . . . Christmas . . . what is Christmas? Just a time for fun, music, and merry-making? Just a time for. . ." Unfortunately, that's all I have left in my addled brain now and, in spite of vigorous internet searches, I've not been able to unearth the piece. But it went on to say, as far as I can recall, that there was much more to Christmas than "fun, music, and merry-making"— that it was a serious time, and children all over the world were dying of starvation while we ate our festive dinners, and even more importantly, people were too focused on worldly pleasures and not enough on the coming of the baby Jesus.

Having been an actor for some years, I can tell you that there is a method to learning lines. One hopes, of course, that lines will be absorbed during the rehearsal process, that the daily running of the lines while working with your fellow actors will instill them in your mind and the movement provided by one's director will also help fix them in place—actors call this "muscle memory"—if I walk over here then this is the line I say; if I pick up this cup, that's the line I say. When all else fails, and most actors hate this, one has to repeat the lines over and over again at home, in the car, at the bank, in the supermarket line, and at the gym, attracting unwelcome attention as passersby think one has gone certifiably crazy.

But I didn't know any of this when I was ten, and clearly neither did Sister Mary. Suddenly, towards the end of the rehearsal process, she told me that I should know my lines by now, and that I was to put down the script. And this is where the trouble really began. Because I honestly had not worked on learning the lines, I'd been given no movement to "fix them in place" and the dear sister had provided me no direction at all. In fact, I'd managed to avoid her focus completely . . . until now. Suddenly, however,

Sister Mary's head spun around like Linda Blair's in *The Exorcist*, and those spiteful eyes glared right at me. I stared right back, wide-eyed with panic, unable to disguise my shock, as the blood drained from my plain freckled face. This was the moment that all her impatience at the younger students, all her frustrations with the fact the play was to be performed on Sunday afternoon and it was nowhere near ready, all her wrath at the sheer thanklessness of her task, came raining down on me. My stomach sank into my scuffed Clarks sandals as I realized I'd transformed from the quiet little girl innocently reading the story on one side of the stage to the object of all her hatred and bile.

A major shift took place in the momentum. Instead of swooping behind me and moving around the little ones, she was abruptly in front of me, standing in the hall and screaming at me, "Move over there!" and "Sit on the step there!" and "Put that script down!" And there I stood—skinny legs quivering, heart thumping, eyes brimming with tears—physically immobilized by fear, abandoned on that vast lonely stage, staring out at my own holy trinity: the two fishes and five loaves high on one side; the crossed keys high on the other; and right in the middle of the parquet floor, forming the third point of the triangle, a very hot, cross nun.

I was afraid to tell my mother about all this. Surely it was a cardinal sin to tell tales about a nun. Anyway, in those days, parents tended to think teachers were right, whatever the circumstances. It's different nowadays. Parents don't seem to support teachers the way they did when I was at school. My mother, a longtime educator herself, retired disillusioned after a mean-spirited parent accused her of abuse when Mum tapped her kid on the head with a pamphlet. But back then, I had no reason to think my mother would believe me if I told her that Sister Mary wasn't being very nice to me. I wouldn't have been at all surprised if my mother said, in response to such an accusation: "Well, dear, I'm sure you deserve it...".

As a result of this new and unwelcome attention, I lived in dread during class that when the afternoon bell rang, I would again be the victim of Sister Mary's anger. I couldn't concentrate on any of my lessons, biting the inside of my lip until it bled, and chewing my nails down to the quick. Worst of all, I seemed unable to learn the lines. Naturally I know now that stark terror can shake the simplest words from one's memory—even as an adult I've found that a nasty director can bully me into forgetting everything I've carefully fixed in my brain—but I didn't know that then, and the more she shouted at me, the more difficult it became for me to utter a single word. Even straightforward reading was tough. All I wanted to do was burst into tears and ask her why she was being so cruel; what had I ever done to her? Couldn't she see from my wobbly lower lip and stuttering that I was desperate to please?

It all came to a head on Friday afternoon, at our last school-day rehearsal before the Sunday show. There was to be a final dress rehearsal on Saturday, but Friday was the last official run-through. I had a costume now: a beautiful, full-length, cream-colored satin dress. It was gorgeous . . . a princess dress, the kind of confection little girls dream of wearing . . . but I couldn't appreciate it because I was in such a state of misery. It didn't help that my long, straight hair had been pulled back off my face in a high, tight pony-tail, so that when I moved my head in either direction, the stretched skin was quite uncomfortable.

Sister Mary had at last given me some basic blocking: move across the stage on this word, point to the manger on this, speak to the audience here, look up at God there. I still wasn't completely sure of my lines and was stumbling all over the place and making stuff up. In the theatre world, we'd call it inspired improvisation; in the land of Catholic nativity plays, it's apparently known as insubordination.

I was supposed to say a particular line, then cross the stage to the other side. But I didn't. I can't recall if I said the line incorrectly or if my muscle memory didn't kick in or if I was so completely petrified that I blanked out, but I remained rooted to the spot like a scared rabbit, not moving when I'd been instructed to. Sister Mary stomped up the steps, grabbed hold of my ponytail and dragged me across the stage to the appropriate place.

Having been tightly gathered, my ponytail was already painful. Add to that the fact that my hair had been in that style for several hours—I think the ladies will back me up here—the skin around my face was sore and aching, and I'd developed a bit of a headache. And then the demon sister had twisted my hair in her hand to get a firm grip. All this combined meant that, when she yanked me into position, I winced in agony. But the real pain I felt was at being so wronged. What had I ever done to this woman? Why did she hate me? I was trying my best to do what she wanted, and it wasn't good enough. I was a failure.

Oh, the anguish of trying not to let her see how much she'd hurt me. As soon as I was released and started the walk home, the lacrimal floodgates opened. "I always thought nuns were supposed to be sweet and kindly," I kept thinking, and I sobbed all the way.

My mother was having a bath when I got home. (I only now question the oddness of her bathing at 4:00 p.m.; I guess single mothers do what they have to do.) It was my usual habit to go into the bathroom and sit on the down-turned toilet-seat lid to tell her about my day, but I didn't want to do that today because she'd see I'd been crying and she'd make me tell her why. When she called out to me to join her, though, there was no way I could say no. I cleaned up my face as best I could, put on a smile and sat down. Alas, you know what it's like when you've been crying, particularly as a kid; it only takes one kind word to set you off again, and my mother immediately noticed my red eyes and asked what was wrong. I didn't want to tell her, felt terrible about grassing on Sister Mary, but I had to share with someone, and who better than my beloved mum? Thus, I explained without much detail, that Sister Mary was angry I hadn't learned my lines and had pulled my hair. I didn't have to say another word.

No one could've been more surprised than I when my mother stood up in the bath, quite naked of course because, well, that's how one takes a bath, and said, "We're going down the school!" You would have to know my mother to apprehend how out of character this was. She was a sweet, peace-loving, mild-mannered woman who hated arguments or confrontations of any kind. To this day, my siblings and I have inherited issues with expressing anger and defending ourselves. You've got to understand, I had never, ever seen this side of my mother before.

In a matter of moments, she was dressed and we were walking back to St. Peter's RC Primary. I use the term "walking" loosely—she *ploughed* through passersby on the street. If my mother had been wearing a crucifix on a chain like Sister Mary, she'd have knocked people into the oncoming traffic with it. She held my hand in a knuckle-cracking grip. I was scared all over again. I literally felt like throwing up; my stomach was doing somersaults. What if Sister Mary denied it, said I'd made it up? If she could torture a little girl, she could certainly lie about her.

We crossed the playground and went through the back entrance of the school, and I'm necessarily fuzzy about the next bit as I think I've blocked it from my memory. If this were a movie, we would storm down the corridor straight to the headmaster's office. But I'm pretty sure we stopped at the first room in the building which was Sister Mary's classroom. I'd like to tell you that I heard my mother say, "If you ever touch my daughter again, I'll have your guts for garters" because that was one of her favorite sayings, but I can't because I don't remember if she went in and partially closed the door, leaving me outside, or if she went in holding my hand. I believe she said something like, "I hear from my child that you pulled her hair and if you ever do something like that again, *(I'll have your guts for garters)* there will be repercussions." Such bravery!

I truly dreaded the next day's final dress rehearsal. However, when I arrived at school, Sister Mary was all smiles, an unfamiliar and intimidating sight. Not one word was said about the meeting with Mum. I was dressed in my lovely angelic outfit and allowed to read from my script while standing stage-left. I kept glancing at the nun, waiting for her to yell at me to move; no instructions came. Lights were set up and music was added. The whole rehearsal went like clockwork, and not a single voice was raised in anything other than joyful Christmas song.

The day came and I was still as anxious as . . . well, as an actress on opening night who has no confidence, who fears her director will make a public display of her if she fails, and who knows her life is over if she flubs a line. (It's every performer's nightmare, frankly. Many of us dream, the night before opening, that we've learned lines to a different play. In my case, I'm usually also wearing an inappropriate costume—I'm Cleopatra when I should be Mary Poppins—that is, if I'm wearing a costume at all; often I'm naked. Once, the play went on around me when I was sitting on a toilet and no one even noticed.) Anyway, I need not have worried about our St. Peter's show. It was spectacular, like a magical dream, with a full house of happy parents watching their adorable children on stage, with glorious Christmas music and a rather surprised ten-year-old narrator. I was given a fresh script which made my many lines much easier to read. You know what? I didn't need it! I mean, it was a great comfort having it in my hand—an angel reading from a divine scroll—but I discovered that, once the bullying was over, I really did know the lines. And I gave a fine performance, which I can say with absolute conviction, as there's no one here to argue otherwise.

I've met other nuns since then, and they've always been just as I envisioned as a child—kind and considerate, and occasionally rather opinionated. As an adult, I was told by a fellow classmate that Sister Mary's order of nuns* chose a path for each one to follow and the path chosen was the one they least wanted to take. If a sister didn't like something, she was going to deal with it by confronting it. Of course, I can't confirm this, but I heard that Sister Mary's most despised thing in the whole wide world was children, that she LOATHED them. According to the rules then, her path was to spend time with children for as long as it took to defeat that demon. And all I have to say to that is . . . well, thanks a bunch!

*See Appendices

40

CHAPTER 6

The Charity Christmas

"At this festive season of the year, Mr. Scrooge, it is more than usually desirable to make some provision for the poor and the destitute who suffer greatly at the present time. Many thousands are in want of common necessaries; hundreds of thousands are in want of common comforts, sir."

I won't launch into a long and rambling monologue about altruism here—that will be a later treat—but I will say this: there are many people in the world who believe that the best thing to do when you're feeling sorry for yourself, when nothing is going your way, is to reach out and offer to do something for others—volunteering your time, talent, and/or hard-earned cash. My mother certainly advocated this view later in life (though she was never sure she had any talent) and definitely instilled in her children a sense of "do unto others as you would have others do unto you." If she held a personal philosophy, kindness was it. If she'd chosen a tombstone to mark her final resting place instead of a copse of oaks in a bluebell wood (where we illegally scattered her ashes, but that's another story), "*BE KIND*" would be italicized upon it.

But it wasn't until she went to college in her early forties to become a teacher and began receiving a regular paycheck that my mother was finally in a position to be generous with her cash. Which leads me to wonder about her unexpected decision when I was about eleven years old to "become benevolent," thereby bringing about a dreadful and much resented episode in our history: the Charity Christmas.

Okay, we weren't indigent, we weren't on the streets. We had shelter and food and clothes (mostly jumble sale, don't get me started) but we were poor enough that we could probably have signed up for charitable assistance ourselves. I mean, our "best clothes" were our school uniforms. We once wore our school uniforms on Christmas Day! And yet, dear Mama suddenly made a Bad Choice, a grim and unpopular decision amongst her children, which rests in infamy to this day: instead of our usual stockings from Father Christmas, our "big" presents, and our splendid festive dinner, we'd give all the money normally spent on those things to the poor.

"What?!" My siblings and I reacted simultaneously, our mouths little O's of dismay, like Japanese anime characters'. "But . . . but . . . *we're* poor!"

St. Peter's RC Church and its accompanying primary school were both big on personal philanthropy. The "need to give" was huge. . . the widow's mite* and all that. There were collection boxes every- where: Caritas, St. Vincent de Paul, Christian Aid, and many others. I'm not criticizing the goal—I absolutely approve of such admirable intentions—but it definitely got rammed down our throats. There was always another country filled with starving kids, another land of drought and desolation, always someone worse off than ourselves. While I accepted that the world was full of desperation and desola- tion, I wasn't entirely convinced there *was* always someone worse off than we were, though I never voiced that aloud. God and my mother would consider me a ghastly child if I complained excessively. It's just that I heard the words "You'll have to do without" often and I was tired of *doing without*. Dad was a staunch Catholic and habitually gave to his local church collection, prompting my mother to say under her breath, "I wish he'd occasionally donate to his wife and children!"

Anyway, the charity de jour was "Biafra," which probably won't mean much to anyone younger than I or who isn't Catholic. In a nutshell, the "Biafran situation" was an international humanitarian relief effort that transported food and medicine to Biafra during the 1967–70 secession war from Nigeria, a.k.a. the Nigerian Civil War*. When my mother talked about giving our Christmas to "the poor," it was actually the Biafrans that she was referring to.

Wearing school uniforms on Christmas Day

From 1st December until the day itself, the Nason kids slid down a slippery slope of disgruntlement as our seasonal traditions were, in our eyes, ruined. To start with, we didn't have an Advent calendar, with or without glitter, because it would've cost valuable cash that we were going to send to Africa. The creche was okay because we already owned it and no fee was required to set it up. We could use our old tree decorations or go walking in the woods free of charge to find more; and I believe, by this time, we owned a little fake Christmas tree, so no expense would be incurred there. Mum went on to use that tree for decades, even after we'd grown up and left. She kept it decorated with the fairy lights securely in place so she could simply yank the yuletide greenery from the little room under the stairs, stick it on a table in the front room window, and plug it in. Never accuse her of not having the Christmas spirit!

That year, breaking my over-sentimental heart, we didn't sit around the washing machine to make the Christmas cake. Big

Bro was likely thrilled about this, as puberty had loomed and he now hated anything connected with his kid sisters. Looking back, I speculate on whether Mum might've been keen to end the precious baking ritual she'd started five years earlier, seeing as we were bigger in size, considerably more argumentative, and no longer fit in the tiny kitchen at the same time. Perhaps the Nason Charity Christmas was a God-given opportunity to make a few changes. If I'm honest with myself, I was always the child who wanted to cling to the old ways—I liked the family unit, however dysfunctional—but perhaps I only longed for it because. . . tradition! Whatever the reason, we never made the cake together again.

On the day itself, the Nason kids eagerly awaited whatever offerings Mum had bought instead of stockings and presents. Even with our awareness that things weren't going to be the same as usual, we were jittery with delight, blood flowing a little faster, hands clenched in anticipation. We regarded each other excitedly. What would Mum have chosen?!

In place of our normal heaps of presents, there was a single large package for the three of us, with a Christmas tag: "Love from Mum." Sis ripped off the wrapping paper—she always made quick work of unwrapping, shredding paper like a playful bear—and there, we found a cardboard box. According to a packing label, it contained plastic "Made in Hong Kong" toys. The box itself looked as if it might actually have travelled across the seas from Hong Kong, all tattered and scrappy. Had it been April Fools' Day rather than Christmas, examining that carton would have been hilarious. As it was, our smiles became somewhat trepidatious as we pulled opened the flaps. "Thanks, Mum!" we said. "This is great!" A strange little frown played on my sister's face; Bro was biting his lip, possibly trying not to laugh. God knows what my face exhibited. Famous for displaying every emotion for the world to witness, I would still have wanted to make Mum happy, but my active mug felt kinda twisted up. Frankly, none of us knew what to think, glancing at each other in puzzlement, trying to mask our disappointment.

Some objects were already broken. Many needed constructing before use, then broke upon use. The toys had the same level of quality as the contents of a Christmas cracker, i.e. cheap and substandard. For some reason, I'm picturing everything as grey-colored but that may be because of my mood at the time. There was an airplane kit; when pieced together the plane flew, but only once before disintegrating. "Oops!" said Bro, putting his hand to his mouth as it crashed to the floor. There was a magnifying glass which, being made of cut-rate plastic, had no magnifying qualities whatsoever. Sis walked about the room, holding it against the door handle, a photo on the wall, and eventually, my face. "It's useless," she whispered to me, crestfallen. "I know," I said, shaking my head in commiseration.

We unpacked a kaleidoscope; metal ring puzzles; miniature games like noughts and crosses (tic-tac-toe), jacks, and tiddly-winks; plastic soldiers and oddly shaped dolls. Detailed online searches have provided nothing to fit my memory of this risible collection.

To give us our due, my cohorts and I graciously pulled each item out of the box, grinning at one another in bemusement—even as our stomachs were sinking at the anticlimax—and managing to sound vaguely excited. "Oh, look at this!" we exclaimed, and "What *is* this?!"

I turned to my mother. "This is fun!" I said, encouraging.

"Oh, good," she replied. "I'm so glad!"

However dejected we might have felt, we kept those slightly less-than-sincere smiles up-front. We desperately wanted to spare Mum any embarrassment. Although it wasn't discussed (that's how we roll in my family), I'm sure, I'm *sure*, she must've been embarrassed. Even if we were flummoxed, we continued to rustle up a show of enthusiasm—"Let's play tiddlywinks, Berni. We can use the coffee table!"—not only playing with the toys, but almost enjoying doing so, laughing at the whole weird situation as we made the best of what we'd been given.

Our Christmas spirits were tested again when, on gather-ing for the seasonal repast, we were met with—instead of turkey and sage-and-onion stuffing—a small chicken in a marshland of soggy veggies. Successful English roast dinners always feature potatoes, roasted in artery-clogging lard until golden brown and crispy on the outside, and fluffy on the inside. I'm convinced those glorious roasted delights were a part of that awful day—Mum couldn't have, wouldn't have, gone so far as to omit the roaspies. Alas, my self-pity is so deep, I don't recall.

After dinner, we went back to our plastic toys, squeezing every ounce of possible amusement out of them. We played until teatime, when mince pies were served—thank God for mince pies, the highlight of the day! At that point, our interest waned or the toys had fallen apart, so we watched TV for the rest of the evening.

In a past filled with dubious Christmases, this one rates highly. It may not seem dire or terrible to most people, in that nothing calamitous happened, but to my siblings and me, it remains noteworthy. Perhaps the simple lack of nice things doesn't seem awfully significant, but when you don't have nice things, or if you never receive the few nice things you're longing for, it can be a huge deal, especially for a child. Wisely, Mum never did it again. To this day, I ponder—my mother being unavailable to ask—if she ended up with enough cash to give to Biafra, or whether this was, in fact, an inspired ruse created because there was no money for Christmas and she couldn't bear to share the same sad story of penury again. Either way, she provided me a gift that wouldn't have crossed her mind at the time. Storytellers wear t-shirts that state "Bad Choices make Good Stories," and this, at least for me, was one for the record books.

See Appendices

CHAPTER 7

I Am the Logjam

"He was made welcome at once, at home within five minutes. Nothing could be heartier. Wonderful party, wonderful friendship, wonderful happiness."

In my ungrateful teens, I did a full one-eighty and turned my churlish back on Mum's old customs. Dissatisfied with the way Christmas was being handled, I had a go at designing and building it for myself . . . outside of the family home.

You see, a number of changes had taken place by the time I turned thirteen in 1970. My fifteen-year-old brother had checked out of the family unit and did his best not to be home at all. He had a girlfriend, and everything connected with her was better than everything connected with us. At the time, I was awfully hurt by his betrayal. It wasn't until I was writing this book that I realized he was simply doing successfully what I hoped I could do. Mum had gone to college and become a teacher. She was also slowly turning vegetarian, and although she still prepared meat dishes for us, traditional roast dinners had all but disappeared, making way for the delights of tofu, nuts, and pulses (legumes), not to mention vegetables of every persuasion. So powerful was the pervasive aroma of boiled cabbage, cauliflower, and Brussels sprouts, even cast-iron sensibilities could be offended. Unless you were a devotee of flatulence in its many guises, our house was a danger-zone. The smell oozing from the kitchen could fell a buffalo. A lit match, and the whole neighborhood would've gone up.

Our father rarely turned up now. When he first left us to live in a rural village on the other side of the country (only ninety miles away, which is nothing to Americans, but quite a distance in UK terms: up to three hours' drive along what were country roads in the 1960s), he'd visit us twice a week, staying for maybe an hour on a Wednesday afternoon or as long as three hours on a Sunday, but never spending the night. I often recorded his visits, or lack thereof, in my journal:

Wednesday, 12 December 1973
Bro's birthday. Daddy wrote and said he'd be home tonight. Funny how we still expect him to come. He didn't.

After he stopped making those regular visits to the family nest, he'd still occasionally pitch up for Christmas, and there was incredible anxiety connected with this: the initial question of whether he'd actually show up; then whether he'd arrive on Christmas Eve or the day itself; then what state he was in, how long he'd stay, and where he would sleep.

Tuesday, 25 December 1973
Daddy got drunk and had to leave the Christmas dinner. He says he's going home tomorrow afternoon. I hope he does.

As we grew older his visits became less frequent; by the time I hit my teens, it was unlikely he'd join us at all. By then, his absence was a relief.

Another thing that had become a habit with us kids was asking Dad for expensive gifts he couldn't possibly afford. When we were little, we weren't aware he had no money, but by the time we were young teenagers, we'd caught on to this, yet we still requested stuff that was beyond his pocket. Maybe we were punishing him for his neglect. Maybe we'd somehow got the idea that he was the one to ask because, God knows, Mum hardly had two pennies to rub together until we were in our late teens. Maybe expensive things equaled love, at least subconsciously (and when I say expensive, I don't mean cars and diamonds; we wanted shoes and bookcases and such). In time, we grasped the stupidity of this. He was a postman in the morning, and worked as an electrical repairman during the day, and a barman at night. Those three jobs gave him sufficient cash to survive. He was in debt much of his life and often had scarcely enough to pay rent on his dilapidated council accommodations*. Later still, I discovered he bought presents on the never-never and took all year to pay for them. He typically gave me feminine things he thought I'd like, rather than what I asked for: dressing gowns, slippers, ornaments, jewelry I'd never wear. Ultimately, my sibs and I got part-time jobs and were expected to fulfill our own material desires. I'd worked a weekend paper-round since I was ten, then took a regular Saturday job at Marks & Spencer, a national retail store, as soon as legally old enough at age fifteen.

Wearing, eating, and holding my Christmas gifts

One year, I specifically asked my dad for a record player—a no-brainer, as he worked in an electrical shop selling and repairing TVs, radios, tape recorders, and the like. Obviously, he'd have access to cheap electrical equipment. "It stands to reason," I said to my sister. "It'll be easy for him." I went on and on about that record player; it was in all my letters to him and every conversation we had. I'd saved my paper-round wages and birthday money to buy the Monkees self-titled first album and we already had "Lovers' Concerto" by the Toys. (We'd asked Dad for an LP by the Supremes; he gave us one by the Toys, another all-black all-female trio, which became one of my all-time favorites.) Anyway, there were now two LPs in my collection and I needed my own turntable.

That year, Dad came home for Christmas. I was never more excited. I spoke about that record player so much, I'd been getting on my brother's nerves, effortless for me because I always got on his nerves. On Christmas morning, I was skipping about, saying, "I'm getting a record player; I know I am. I just know it!" and Bro hissed right in my face, "Why don't you shut up! You're irritating me already. You always spoil everything!" On a normal day, that might've made me cry, but not that day. I was sure that record player was mine because I'd talked of nothing else. And there was indeed a massive gift among the "big presents"—I'd seen Dad bring it in—so I had a really good feeling.

When it came time to open, I noticed that the large package was not in my gift area. It was conspicuously absent. One by one, we opened our presents, and it still hadn't materialized. Then it appeared and was placed . . . in my younger sister's pile. I was struggling to smile now, but I was certain he'd magically produce an equally large package and set it in my area. However, my stomach dropped when Sis took her turn before me in the present opening lineup and she unwrapped, lo and behold, a lovely record player— obviously second-hand, but still lovely. I felt my face twist into a perplexed frown. Sis looked at me, eyes round with alarm, understanding what I must be feeling. I shook my head, disbelieving. A sharp pain that I now recognize as grief stabbed my chest area. My chin was already wobbling and I pinched my lips together in an effort not to cry as I picked up the last present in my pile, an envelope. It contained 10 pounds sterling, a lot of money for Dad to give his child, but not enough to buy a record player. All was lost. I shot a look of bewilderment at my mother, who was regarding me closely, inscrutable, before I excused myself to use the loo. Mum followed me into the dining room, where my tears gushed, no stopping them.

"How could he?" I said quietly. "He knew it was what I wanted. How could he give it to Sis?"

"I'm sure he just got muddled up," she said, her lips a line of disapproval. I was baffled. Disapproval of me or Dad? Did she empathize with me or not? Surely she was on my side. But her expression was unreadable. "I expect he forgot which of you asked."

"But . . . but he *had* to know it was me. I've been asking for months. We *discussed* it! How could he forget?"

"You mustn't say anything, Berni. Not a word. Understand?" It wasn't clear if Mum felt sorry for me or not, but right before my eyes, she took control of whatever emotions she was experiencing. Her face hardened and her very British stiff upper lip took over. "We don't want to spoil the day, do we?"

And so nothing was ever said. I didn't want to spoil the day, even though it was spoiled for me. Any show of anguish on my part would be considered "wallowing in it" so I cleaned up my face and didn't mention that my heart was broken, not because I didn't get a record player, but because my father had forgotten it was I who'd asked for it. Mum didn't bring it up either. She never told Dad, as far as I know, that he'd made a mistake. That's how it was in our house. Absolutely no rocking the boat, absolutely no discussion that could've set an awkward situation straight.

To give my little sister her due, she came into our bedroom later and said, "You can use it any time you want. It'll be our record player. I didn't want it. I'd rather have got the ten pounds." Bless her! For the life of me, I can't recall if I gave her the money—I hope I did—but I certainly used that record player as if it were mine until I could afford to get another with my own money.

I think that was the last time our dad came home for the Holidays (maybe Mum did have a word with him), and the following year, my brother, who clearly couldn't bear the prospect of another Christmas Day with his sisters, spent it with his girlfriend. Thus began my endeavor, throughout my teenage years, to arrange my own festivities, which involved getting invited to other people's houses and enjoying time with their families, because it was only my family that was troublesome. I was especially attracted to other people's families (OPFs) if there was a boy involved, mistakenly believing that having a Christmas Beau would automatically provide a Joyeux Noel. Mon Dieu, quelle imbécile!

I must say, it seemed at first that I might be correct, that OPFs had better celebrations than we did. OPFs treated me, their guest, with such courtesy and kindness that I felt valued . . . *cherished* . . . a singular sensation for me. However, bit by bit, I came to detect cracks in their armor, family flaws that were hidden from me precisely because I was a guest. Having an outside visitor for a formal family dinner can make an enormous difference to your relatives' behavior—haven't you noticed? In the end, I was forced to admit that things were the same for everyone, that is, wanting the Day to be fabulous, trying extra hard not to shout at siblings or get irritable with parents, etc. I was still too immature to understand that a successful event rarely has much to do with superficial trappings and a lot more to do with how a person feels and what they bring to the occasion. I (and others too, it would appear) tried to force the situation, instead of relaxing and relishing the moment. Hold on a minute . . . you mean I was part of my problem instead of the victim of circumstances? Hmm. Now there's an idea.

Oddly, I have almost no recollection of my two Christmases as a young married woman. Wait . . . what? I haven't told you about my adventure of being a young married woman yet? Oh, dear. Well, if I'm keeping this in any kind of order, then I suppose you should know that, in my late teens, I did in fact meet a charming man, accept his kind offer of marriage, and decide to settle down. It doesn't take a genius or therapist or kindergartner to determine that I was creating a clan of my own, having exhausted attempts to mold my natural kinfolk to fit my idea of what a family unit should look like. Charlie and I only lasted two years, though we remained friends for a long time afterwards. In our defense, we loved each other—I certainly loved him; he was the first man I ever loved—but I imagine we were both inclined to ignore our many dissimilarities. At that time, he was looking to settle down in the old-fashioned way with a traditional wife, house, car, job, then kids. I thought I wanted the same, until it became clear that I was the traditional wife in the scenario, and the house/car/job/kids were all that might be on offer. Then I was through the door and sprinting down the road quicker than he could say, "What's for dinner, darling?"

While I'd love to regale you with amusing stories of our Holiday exploits as a couple, there's a gap in my reminiscences—"The Lost Christmases," I call them. I stopped writing a real journal as soon as I got married, keeping only general calendar notes, but what I put down implies that Charlie and I carried out stocking and present rituals in our newlyweds' house (in Bishopstoke, not far from Winchester). My calendar also suggests visits with my mum, then his parents. The first year, it looks as if his mum and dad came to our family home for the afternoon dinner. Dad and Bro didn't attend, but it appears that Sis and boyfriend came along. Charlie and I might have gone to the pub, which was becoming popular at that time. We may have worked on Christmas Eve, as he was a bartender at the King Alfred and I, at the South Western. Sadly, it's all a bit of a blank. Either way, there were two Christmases before the marriage ended, and then, at the age of twenty-two, I had to start over.

Not long after I'd moved back in with my mum, a new family dynamic emerged. Dad began a peculiar tradition of visiting our family home on Christmas Eve, and not alerting us in advance. He'd leave a box of gifts under the front steps, outside the cellar, then return to his distant home. His Santa impersonation usually backfired because the box was not visible as you approached the house and we sometimes didn't find the presents until the New Year. This went on for years. "Please tell us in future when you're planning to swing by," we'd say, "so we can see you." Eventually, one year, he told us to expect him, and we gathered a box of festive goodies to give him in exchange. I found intense joy in choosing a tweedy-green lambswool sweater from our local Debenhams department store. Wrapping it carefully, it cheered me to think he'd have a present from me to open on Christmas morning. He didn't show up. The gift box stayed outside the cellar door for weeks waiting for him to come, but he never did, and it was never discussed because, as you know, that's how it was in our family. From that point on, we were lucky if we received a Christmas card from him. I kept and wore that sweater for years. I still have it.

There was one occasion during my mid-twenties where I witnessed (with my prematurely jaded eyes) a person getting it right . . . and a most unlikely person, at that. Sis and I accepted an invitation to a mutual friend's place for Christmas Day tea. We didn't particularly want to go, but couldn't think of a reason not to. "It might be fun," we said, our aloof expressions suggesting otherwise. "It probably won't be," we agreed, deadpan, "but there's nothing else going on." Having had a dull, unexceptional day so far, we had no expectations. Also, to be honest, Len— about same age as I, living in his own flat in a big old house nearby— didn't seem like the sort who'd put together much of a social gathering. Poorly educated and working a menial job, he could be a bit of a lout. He was often in trouble for saying what he thought to the wrong people at the wrong time—I'd seen him more than once with a black eye. He was what one might call a "yobbo," swearing like a trooper and drinking beer and whisky as if Prohibition were on its way back (we knew him from the local pub). But none of that mattered because, despite the black marks against his name, we really liked him. He was kind and hilariously funny . . . always considered to have a way with words, whether it got him in trouble or not. For Sis and me, those qualities made up for the rest of his foibles. Anyway, the plan was to drop in for half an hour and fulfill our obligation before making our excuses, should we find ourselves bored.

Our very reluctance meant we were pleasantly surprised to note that Len had made a *proper* English tea, including Earl Grey made in a teapot (served in teacups) and mulled wine. There was also, of course, loads of beer in the fridge. It being Christmas, Sis and I chose alcohol over tea. Handing us our wineglasses, Len said,

"What can I offer you lovely ladies? Ya gotta start with sarnies before you go on to the cake. That's the rule in our house and I'm stickin' with it."

"It's our mother's rule too," I said, looking at the spread neatly laid out on a table: several plates of sandwiches, cut in triangles, along with mince pies and Christmas cake. "What kind of sarnies did you make?"

"There's egg and cress—that's why the place smells of me ol' dad's farts. And there's . . . oh fuck, I've forgotten." He reached out, snatched a sandwich from one of the plates, and pulled it open to check inside. "Oh, yeah. Salmon spread and cucumber." Then he pressed the sandwich back together and replaced it on the plate, fingerprints clearly visible. Noticing my eyes question this action, he grabbed the sandwich. "Shit, sorry; I'm always forge'in' me manners," and he shoved the entire white bread triangle into his mouth. Now he was unable to talk, though that didn't stop him trying.

"Made the mince pies meself, this mornin'," he mumbled. "Pleased wiv 'em, I am. When you've 'ad a coupla sarnies, tuck in, girls, tuck in!"

"What about the cake?" I said. "Did you make that?"

Len positively beamed. "'Course I bloody did. I know what yer thinkin', ladies—'Len can bake cakes?'—but ya can't judge a book its cover, can ya? It's me ma's recipe. Did a better job than she did, I can tell ya. When me bruvvers come over later, *they'll* tell ya. I'm a bloody good cook, I am, better than me mum. *She'll* tell ya!"

By this time, Sis and I were both giggling. We helped ourselves to sandwiches, and settled on the sofa. The other guests said hello before going back to their conversations. As I nibbled my egg-and-cress sarnie, which was delicious, Sis leaned over. "No question of it," she said. "He's got a way with words." I did a spit-take across the room.

I took in my surroundings. The flat was nothing special, just a few rooms in someone else's big old house, yet it was comfortable and snug, with warm lighting, gentle seasonal music, and a decorated tree in the window. Len himself was so relaxed, so convivial as he welcomed more friends, with his broad local accent and genuine words of welcome, that I was immediately comfortable, which was unusual for me. "Ya can't judge a book by its cover," I mused.

In retrospect, I note that Len's trappings were simple and basic, but I don't think it would've mattered if he'd presented nothing more than a packet of salt & vinegar crisps. His cordiality, the warmth of his hospitality, his *sincerity* was what counted. And my own lack of expectation meant that I was open to whatever came my way. I was content in that moment. More than that, I was happy. Happy! Was I conscious of that at the time? I doubt it. Because it was a while yet before I understood that genuine pleasure has little to do with festive frills, and—here it is again—everything to do with the cordiality, hospitality, and sincerity I received, and whatever I chose to tender in return. I was too wrapped up in personal dysfunction to understand it then, still learning that I always tried too hard to make things go the way I wanted, instead of lightening up and going with the flow. I blocked the flow. I built a logjam in the flow. Oh, no! I *was* the logjam!

See Appendices

CHAPTER 8

The Mayor's Christmas Carols

"Foggier yet, and colder! Piercing, searching, biting cold. A carol singer, gnawed and mumbled by the hungry cold as bones are gnawed by dogs, stooped down at Scrooge's keyhole to regale him with a Christmas carol: but at the first sound of 'God bless you, merry gentleman! May nothing you dismay!' Scrooge seized the ruler with such energy of action, that the singer fled in terror, leaving the keyhole to the fog and even more congenial frost."

D on't you love a good Christmas carol? I'm not being sarcastic. Doesn't it just lift your spirit? Come on, ya miserable gits, stop shaking your heads. You may be dubious about other Christmas practices, but you gotta love belting out a jolly old carol! All that bleak midwinter, that lullay lullay, those maids a-milkin' and lords a-leapin'. Okay, okay, I get you; I understand. But my mum wouldn't have. She absolutely adored carol singing, so it was always an enormous feature of our December agenda. Although we sang a variety at St. Peter's Church throughout Advent, there would be only one or two per mass, and Mum wanted a whole bunch of them, one after another. Consequently, she always took us to the Mayor's Christmas Carol Concert that took place annually in early December; it was part of her ongoing bid to ensure that Baby Jesus season wasn't a complete washout, what with dear Papa's absence and all.

The mayor's caroling event was a public affair, held in Winchester Guildhall at the Broadway, which is at the end of the High Street, close to what would've been the east gate of the City, if the gate had still existed. Easier to say, it was at the bottom of "down town," close to King Alfred's statue (affectionately called "King Alfie") and the Old Mill on the River Itchen.

Our home was maybe a mile's walk from the Guildhall, but I imagine it must've taken Mum at least an hour to get there, three small kids in tow. Bro, elder by two years, preferred to walk ahead so he could pretend not to know us. As the middle child, I'd do anything I could to be helpful and not to be nuisance. Sis, one year younger than I, was disgruntled about everything and was usually dragged along like a screaming, blonde, curly haired Eeyore.

From our house, we'd go up St. Paul's Hill, past St. Paul's Church, which later became Mum's church of choice after she reverted to the Church of England, the religious persuasion of her youth. Her conversion to Catholicism in order to marry our father had caused acrimony and umbrage in her own family, and Dad's private display of Catholicism-in-action didn't align with her own concept of true spiritual ethics.

We'd walk across the bridge over the main London-Bournemouth-Weymouth railway line, always stopping to look back at Winchester Railway Station. As a kid, I could just about see through the railings above the mossy brick wall, if I stood on tiptoe. Sis had to be lifted up. It was always more exciting if a train steamed by as we crossed, especially if it was the through-train from London to Bournemouth, which didn't stop at the station. This mechanical dragon would whoosh beneath us, and if we were really lucky, the monster would shriek, snorting its poisonous white breath through the black metal railings. It was simultaneously thrilling and terrifying. I missed those steam trains when they disappeared from British Rail's rolling stock.

Then we'd walk through the Westgate of the City of Winchester, through which there's a clear view of the High Street with the town clock, and the green roof of the Guildhall, and St. Giles Hill beyond. All we had to do now was walk the length of the High Street, past the 15th-century City Cross, known to Wintonians as the Buttercross, where people came in olden days to sell their produce, to reach the Guildhall*.

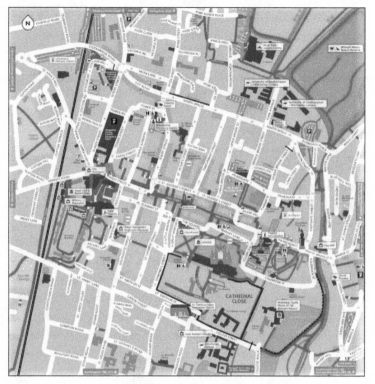

Winchester Sightseeing Map
courtesy Ontheworldmap.com

Mum was ruthless in her review. "Such an ugly building! Victorian architecture is hideous; far too many bells and whistles!" she'd said, baffling me because there were no bells or whistles that I could see. Historians are kinder and describe its facade as "relatively uncluttered," with four statues of kings and bishops with Winchester connections, as well as panels showing major events in the city's history. The panel below the clock-tower shows Winchester's mythical first mayor, Florence de Lunne, receiving the city's charter from King Henry II. It is right to describe her as "mythical"—I haven't discovered a single thing about this woman. How did there come to be a female mayor in the 12th century? Mum would've known the answer.

A while back, the building's interior had been all gussied up when it was reinvented as a wedding and conference venue, but in my lifetime it was used for everything from church bazaars to psychic fairs. It's been the town art school and police station, and it currently houses the Tourist Information Centre beneath its majestic entrance, which I visited a thousand times after Mum became a tourist guide. There's always been a tea shop, of course, because it's in England.

The carol service became an annual event in our young lives, and even when Mum stopped taking us because we were old enough to make our own choices, I still went along each year. I preferred to attend with Mum because, although she gave me too many instructions and sang embarrassingly, excruciatingly loudly, we could make each other laugh at the drop of the hat. Mum was Queen of Comedic Asides, a wisecracker extraordinaire, the Dorothy Parker of Elm Road. The carol concert was ripe with mini episodes at which to poke fun. Our favorite moments were when bored children misbehaved, belligerent drunks behaved worse, and seniors nodded off in spite of the din. We giggled uncontrollably at the latter: *how could they fall asleep during such a rollicking racket?* We especially appreciated individuals whose singing voices were particularly strident. Did Mum get the irony? We'll never know.

There was an orchestra, a local choir, and usually some choir boys from Winchester College (known as quiristers), famous for singing in the Cathedral in their flawless, high, unbroken voices. Some carols were sung by just the choir, some by just the choir boys, and some by everyone. Even when I was enjoying the others performing, I could hardly contain myself as I eagerly anticipated another chance join in. My mother was obviously the same, although she regularly sang when she wasn't supposed to—mortifying to my teenage sensibilities. It's an extremely irritating habit, and I know this because I do it myself. (I was once asked to move to the upper balcony at the Austin Paramount Theatre when I persisted in singing every word of every song in *Seven Brides for Seven Brothers* during their Summer Film Series. The kind usher said simply, "If you move up there," pointing to the nosebleed seats, "you can sing as loudly as you want and no one will be able to hear you." I did so and she was right, and I was as happy as a pig in swill.)

There was a conductor who did double-duty as emcee. I've no memory of conductors from earlier years, only recalling that in my eyes they simply waved their hands crazily for no apparent reason. "I could easily do that," I thought on more than one occasion. Our favorite conductor was Julian Smith, director of chapel music at Winchester College from 1977 until 1992. He led us, the dumb public, in "In the Bleak Midwinter." "Now this verse is just for the women—gentle; this one, just for the men—powerful; this one, just for the children. Sing quietly now, children." One of my favorites was "The Twelve Days of Christmas," which got faster and faster as we went along, the jolly crowd bursting into breathless delighted laughter at the end.

Finally, the climax of the whole standing-room-only event was "Hark, the Herald Angels Sing." Julian Smith encouraged the public to give it their all; to leave nothing behind. I tried to hear myself over everyone else. Everyone was obviously doing the same thing, trying to be noisier than their neighbors. I'd get swept up in each thrilling verse, getting louder and more raucous. I'd always sing so wildly and with such abandon that I almost fainted. Every year, I looked forward to that moment . . . not the hyperventilation, because that's horrid, but the joyful, exuberant noise. One year, Julian Smith conducted so enthusiastically, his hands a mad flurry of motion, that his baton snapped in two, and the broken half flew up into the balcony. Everyone laughed heartily, including the orchestra, and the music came to a standstill to bring order to the chaos. One of the mayor's children found the baton bit and threw it back down, causing even more hysteria. Of course, then we had to start the last verse again with Mr. Smith using just half a baton. It was hilarious. Mum and I went along the following year and, on the last section of "Hark, the Herald Angels Sing," it happened again. Once more, the audience fell into fits of laughter and once more, Mr. Smith had to wait for calm so he could restart the final chorus. Oh, it was splendid! To this day, when I hear that carol, tears flow immediately, bypassing my head entirely, going straight to my heart.

It was the carol service of December 1981 that takes the prize for my most memorable attendance. It was my last, as well. By this time, I'd reverted to Mum's original traditions (my own plans not having had much success) and participated with or without friends or family because it was, after all, tremendous fun. Christmas wasn't Christmas without it.

I was twenty-four years old and having an *annus horribilis*, as our dear old queen would have put it . . . a very horrible year indeed. After my early marriage had failed and I'd got divorced, I fell in love with, broke up with, got back together with, then decided to break up forever with the man I honestly believed was the love of my life—all because my friends said they didn't think he was right for me. Having read Jane Austen's *Persuasion* in high school, you'd think I'd know better, wouldn't you? Dear Jane, patron saint of Winchester, in spite of your wise words to the contrary, I was persuaded. No learning from others' mistakes for me; I need to fall off life's tightrope into the fetid, stinky water myself. That breakup was a mistake from which I suffered all through the year (and in years to come, as it happens, but let's not dwell). It looks ridiculous in writing but my life was a bit like a sad, sorry, shamefully pathetic version of *The Bachelorette* or a single woman's version of *The Housewives of Orange County* called *The Unmarriageable Spinsters of Winchester City*. Thus, when I met "rebound man" (let's call him "Dave the Shithead") who was absolutely the wrong man for me and to whom I should never have given the time of day, I let myself believe I cared, and allowed him to treat me appallingly.

England in 1981 was no picnic either. Margaret Thatcher, the dreaded Iron Lady herself, was prime minister; the Social Democratic Party was formed; there were parcel bombs and domestic terrorism and hunger strikes by Irish Republican Army prisoners; the Ford Cortina was the most popular car for the tenth year in a row (have you *seen* the Ford Cortina?); Prince Charles got engaged to, then married Lady Diana Spencer, and we all know how that turned out. Then, in December, adorning the year with a thick layer of metaphorical icing on the cake, the UK experienced its coldest temperatures and heaviest snowfall since the infamous Big Freeze of 1962–63. Remember Chapter 2?

The snow and cold began on 8th December and, according to my research, continued until after Christmas, though we didn't, of course, have snow on Christmas Day, which would've been the right thing to do—actualized icing on the cake. Oh, no, that wasn't going to happen. Couldn't happen. This is Great Britain. Thanks a lot, Great British weather. F***ing it up, as usual.

(I have mixed feelings about snow. Like folks the world over, I rejoice at the first snowfall. I walk in it, and wax lyrical over its white, ethereal beauty. Then, the very moment it gets dirty and slushy, I hate it and whine about it and long for spring. In my opinion, snow should have a four-hour lifespan. Yes, you're white and frosty and cute. Now bog off and make way for the crocuses and daffs.)

For some inexplicable reason—and this says something about my misery at the time—I haven't got a diary note of which Sunday the carol concert took place. This may be because Dastardly Dave had been persuaded by his best friend/housemate, Alan, to invite me over, following the carol service, and cook me a Christmas dinner to make up for his multiple betrayals with other ladies. I had little faith that the meal would happen—his previous conduct suggested he was unreliable—and I dreaded it in case I discovered that I was, yet again, a gullible idiot.

Our UK weather forecasters had warned that a snowstorm was on its way and to be prepared. When I left the house, it was freezing already, so I was tightly bundled up. I'd always read that conditions warmed up a bit before it snowed on account of the cloud cover, because obviously you need to have clouds for there to be precipitation, and by the time I walked through the Westgate at the top of town, the sky was totally grey—that spooky surreal kind of grey that says trouble is brewing—and teeny weeny flakes were starting to fall, nothing much, but enough for me to pull up the hood of my coat. It didn't get much worse until I was nearly at the Guildhall. Then the winter heavens opened and down it came, thick chunky flakes that settled immediately. In spite of my personal gloom, this fresh virgin snow was pleasing, and as we hadn't reached 25th December yet, I permitted myself to believe we might have that longed-for white Christmas.

Streams of families were climbing the concrete steps into the building, heads down, braving the white sheets of winter. When I met a friend, Grace, in the Guildhall lobby, we gushed about the weather and how Christmassy it would be to enjoy carols under such ideally festive circumstances. Grace and her little boy, whose eyes were cartoon saucers of excitement, were both enjoying the event for the first time, and the wintry feeling only increased the charm. The improbability of Jesus's being born in such a storm, since Bethlehem winters rarely had snow, never entered our minds.

I'm almost sure the concert began with "I Saw Three Ships" and, at some point, we touched on "Away in a Manger" (English-style, of course, with a different melody from the US) and "Once in Royal David's City." Within a very short time, all my troubles were packed up in my old kit bag, and I was grinning fit to burst.

When you live in a damp, drafty place like the British Isles, you take for granted that inescapable musty smell of damp overcoats and wet raincoats, the sight of dripping umbrellas on the backs of chairs and under seats. If one is lucky enough to be in a heated building (not a done deal in old British buildings, as many of you well know) one can almost see the steam rising from human bodies; the fusty smell is all-pervasive. It's just the way it is. On that snowy day at the mayor's carol concert, with all those bodies pressed together* singing merrily, I actually did notice it—I could almost see the mildew forming—and yet, I didn't mind one bit. The unmitigated joy of song totally outweighed the discomfort of the stale tinned-sardine experience. People coughed and sneezed; cold and flu germs danced jigs of delight as they bounced from one malodorous person to the next. It simply didn't matter. In those euphoric moments, if anyone noticed anything untoward, no one cared.

The snow continued to fall heavily; one could see it through the tall, churchlike, perpendicular-style windows. The main hall was so packed that our wrinkled programs (which doubled as song sheets) had to be shared, held by damp, gloved hands between pairs of people. We were well into the event when there was a barely audible clap of thunder from outside the building. This may well have been preceded by a streak of lightning, though I didn't see one. What I did hear immediately afterwards was a cracking sound from inside the building. Then, seconds later, all the lights went out. In the pitch black, they were cries of "Oh!" and "Whoa!", even a few small screams, and a lone voice, saying "Oops!". Right away, flashlights were switched on, and there may even have been a generator because, if memory serves, a few old-fashioned lanterns came on to cast a dim glow. The conductor asked everyone to remain calm and patient as ushers and volunteers lit candles, and placed them upon whatever surfaces they could find. Small candles were held by audience members, too. I suppose it must've been a major fire hazard, but it meant nothing to me then.

Photo credit: Hampshire Chronicle

Within a fraction of time, we were ready to recommence. As snowflakes tumbled past the arched windows in the flickering candlelight, the orchestra fired up again. Now the singing was even more enthusiastic than before. I felt as if I'd been swept back in time, when simple things had greater significance: light in the dark, warmth in the cold, glorious song in the cheerless days of winter. Suddenly, I was in olde-worlde England. When I closed my eyes, unexpected tears seeped from the outer edges, and my voice wobbled so that I could hardly add it to the happy choir. And when I opened them, oh, the faces of my fellow Wintonians! If they'd been happy before, now they were gleeful, euphoric, and when we got to "Hark, the Herald Angels Sing," you can only imagine the unbridled rapture. Magic was created that afternoon.

By the time we left the building, the Broadway was as completely iced as the finest Christmas cake, the proverbial picture postcard. A snowy carpet covered the ground and everything, from red Royal Mail letterboxes to City of Winchester garbage cans, was dressed in white winter clothes, topped with a crisp sparkling snow-beret. In the yellow light of the old-fashioned lampposts swirled burly white feathers. If God or Mother Nature or Father Christmas hadn't planned this for me to savor, then how, who? I couldn't be cynical, I just couldn't. I waved goodbye to Grace and her son, slipped through the bustling crowds, and made my way to Dishonorable Dave's.

As anticipated, he wasn't there; he'd gone to his parents' place without calling me to cancel. Perhaps I should've checked in advance, but you know how it is; I was afraid he'd confirm what I already dreaded.

I was definitely sad to be so disrespected by a man who had claimed to love me, but this story doesn't have quite the woeful end you might expect. I was so lighthearted from the enchanting concert that I took the bad news in stride. Also, Despicable Dave's housemate, Alan, was so upset with his old schoolfriend that he and his girlfriend prepared the entire Christmas dinner, from punch to plum pudding, and entertained me themselves. We raised our punch glasses and toasted: "To the season!" and "To the snow!" and "To absent friends!" which made us all laugh. Alan said, "He's a dickhead; he doesn't know what he's missing!" Then, grateful for these kind surrogates, I vowed to end the toxic romance (I did) and tucked into my turkey.

*See Appendices

CHAPTER 9

Do They Know It's Christmas?
(adapted from *Tea in Tripoli*, 2017)

"Much they saw, and far they went, and many homes they visited, but always with a happy end. The Spirit stood beside sick beds, and they were cheerful; on foreign lands, and they were close at home; by struggling men, and they were patient in their greater hope; by poverty, and it was rich. In almshouse, hospital, and jail, in misery's every refuge, where vain man in his little brief authority had not made fast the door, and barred the Spirit out, he left his blessing, and taught Scrooge his precepts."

D ecember 1984 found me living and working in North Africa, trying to find "a new me" and asking myself an important question: "Should I spend Christmas in Libya?" And much to my surprise, I found myself answering: "Why not?" Maybe it was time to experience it in another place, from a unique perspective, with a different attitude. I had never spent the season anywhere other than in my family home, and there hadn't been a Christmas Day on which I'd missed church in my twenty-seven years of life, although to be fair, it was by now the only day on which I regularly attended. I had become what good Catholics call a Christmas Catholic.

Christmas in a Muslim country is weird. Some of the more capitalist areas with a broader view of the world welcomed the event because it brought in tourists, but Libya wasn't one of them. The practice of Christianity was permitted and there were a few churches in Tripoli, but there was absolutely no visible acknowledgement of any Christian events.

To be honest, I had no desire to return home to Winchester for the holiday. Although the previous Christmas hadn't been unpleasant, I felt disconnected from the idea of a traditional yuletide. I'd been in Tripoli nearly a year; England and my family seemed remote. I'd broken up with my last boyfriend, Ian, via snail-mail, so he certainly wouldn't welcome me; he'd acrimoniously moved out of my flat, leaving it empty and uninviting. I didn't tell my mother my reservations about returning, and I kept up a running correspondence on the subject, which caused me frequent pangs of guilt. I'd obtained permission to take time off, even bought a ticket, but I gave myself the option to choose last-minute.

3 December 1984
Dear Mum,

I wish I could feel even the slightest bit festive. It is a little colder here in the mornings and late at night, but during the day, we can still walk around in short sleeves with a jumper tied around the neck, just in case. The sun still shines most of the time—I don't mind that—I just can't get used to not wearing scarf and gloves. It's hard to psych myself up for Christmas here.

As already mentioned, I'd read Charles Dickens' *A Christmas Carol* annually since I was a teen, and now, in early December 1984, I grabbed my scruffy copy and read it at lunchtime to try to get myself in the mood. Weather permitting, I sat on the office roof as the mosques blared out the call to prayer, while Arab life teemed around me. Every now and then, I pulled myself from the pages of Scrooge and the ghosts in snowy Dickensian London to glance over the neighboring rooftops: women hanging out laundry, children playing with goats, babies crawling on colorful rugs. It occurred to me that the simplicity of life in Tripoli in the 1980s was not unlike that of London in the 1880s—apart from the goats, that is, and the rugs . . . and the weather.

That year, *A Christmas Carol* did not weave its usual spell. I was bonkers to think that reading that book alone might do it.

The absence of familiar things—festive lights in Winchester High Street, cheerfully decorated shop windows, the mayor's Christmas carols, choral singing in our world-famous cathedral, midnight mass at St. Peter's RC—became more and more unbearable as my December limped along.

The expat community, especially the families, undoubtedly came up with brilliant ideas on how to celebrate the season in that barren, forlorn land. There was a Catholic church, so I'm sure there were Advent services and carol singing too. Did I investigate? No, it was all too much trouble. I just wanted Christmas to "happen." But I was hanging around with a bunch of young male geologists the same age as I, who could build a bar out of orange crates, brew the finest beer and wine in the (dry) land, and didn't have a clue about creating Christmas.

On the day that my *new* boyfriend, Giovanni (have you lost count yet? It's only two boyfriends so far in this chapter!) flew to his Italian home for Christmas and the New Year, my adventurous alter ego pulled me up by my ear. "Stop whining, Berni!" it said, sharply. "Stop it! This isn't just going to happen. It's up to you to *find* some festive feeling." I got the message and took up the search for a Christmas tree. *What?* I hear you say. *In Libya?* Yes, there are conifers growing in North Africa, in Libya even, but you know what? There wasn't a Christmas tree lookalike to be found. I wasn't expecting shops selling them—"Fayed's Famous Fir Trees!"—when it was hard to find even everyday items for normal life, but I had thought there might be a tiny tree in a front yard somewhere that I could "borrow." Or that someone might have a fake fir tree, or something I could make resemble one. But apparently, if an expat had made the effort to bring a fake tree into the country, they either held on to it until they left, so as to sell it on the black market for thousands of dollars, or it had to be pried from their cold dead hands like Charlton Heston's gun.

I thought: *What would my mum do?* I obviously couldn't ask her because I hadn't told her I might not be flying home. Instead, I imagined her voice in my head. *Why don't you make a Christmas tree out of a cardboard box, darling? I know you can.* My brother is a gifted artist and my sister, a wizard with a sewing machine, but I'm not famous for my crafty ways. Still, necessity is the mother of invention. If I build a tree, Christmas will come!

Cardboard was not available for purchase, nor was paper—Libya was the land of "not available," so I wasn't surprised. I nabbed a few empty boxes from the local souk but that cardboard was too thick. After a fruitless search, friends and work colleagues stepped up, donating green craft paper, kitchen scissors, (brought from England; all I had were nail scissors), a stapler and a few staples. I myself had the remainder of a roll of kitchen foil, about 6 inches left of a mini-roll of Scotch tape, and some scraps of colored paper, snipped from *Time* and *Newsweek.*

I set it all out one evening and, with a large glass of home-brewed rice wine in hand—booze was obviously "not available" in Libya, so we made our own—I regarded my diverse bits and pieces, mentally designing. Then I went to work. I folded and marked, cut and shaped, stapled and taped, tweaked and crafted. I felt like the shoemaker's wife, making clothes for the elves. I was the brave little tailor, working against the odds, seven in one stroke! I was Dolly Parton's mama with her coat of many colors! I was *Project Runway*, Christmas Tree Edition!

My finished work was a masterpiece: a fabulous tree, boasting hearts and bells. I went all out on my vision and made a silver foil angel, sporting a white net cape for wings. Don't ask where the netting came from; no idea. A Christmas miracle! The tree was too flimsy to support the angel so, with a bit of yellow paper, I styled a fierce pointy star to grace the top. Eventually, the joyfully fabricated, magnificently ornamented tree was ready. With great pride and due ceremony, I took it to the office and placed it, angel alongside, on my bookcase.

My Italian and Arab coworkers looked at my work of art, and asked, almost without exception, "Che cos'è?" meaning *What is it?* When my boss passed through, he stopped, looked, and chuckled. "Ah, Bernadetta, Bernadetta," he said, smiling. Then, as he disappeared into his own office, he shook his head and said what sounded like "Assolutamente demenziale," which, loosely translated, means:

She's barking mad. Perhaps I misheard him. But I'd made the effort, my spirits were lifted, and I walked around the office, singing, "It's beginning to look a lot like Christmas, here in Tripoli."

This black-and-white picture does not do it justice!

But all semblance of seasonal jollity disappeared shortly thereafter, when a jovial group of us went to visit two British pals, Cindy and Heather, at their apartment. Since they'd invited us to a little holiday party and we were therefore expected, the lack of response to our persistent knocking was odd. After puzzling on the doorstep for a while, we gave up. Several phone calls later, one of my geologist pals, Ben, announced that our friends, both dental nurses, had been attacked at knifepoint and were "in custody." My anxiety engine, which, with the distractions of a new home, new boyfriend, and renewed interest in Christmas, had been idling along happily, immediately revved back into action, and shifted into high gear. The full terrifying story was that two Libyan youths had brutalized and sexually assaulted the girls, having broken into their villa in the middle of the night. This is their story, not mine, so I'll leave it at that.

Suffice to say, my recent decision to live alone in a neighborhood where I didn't know a soul now appeared rash and reckless.

Whatever were you thinking? And the concept of a Tripoli Christmas suddenly struck me as alarming, too. *Are you insane?* Everything was tipping the balance in favor of a speedy withdrawal from my self-made deal, when a plausible deal-breaker materialized as if from nowhere.

I knew it could be rainy, but when you're that close to the Sahara Desert and you've experienced temperatures that fry your skin, you forget about the cold and wet. In mid-December 1984, Libya broke with its tradition of winter rainfall lasting "several days," and it rained continuously for over a week. With roads in such poor condition, rainfall led to subsidence and flooding. Cars hydroplaned off the street; wadis (dry riverbeds) filled to capacity. Roads were impassable, so even darts contests and video nights at friends' villas, which were really my only regular entertainments, were unreachable. Isolated in my suburban villa where streets were knee-deep in water, I felt marooned. 'Twas not the season to be jolly at all.

There you have it. In spite of my inexplicable desire to remain in Libya, I reconfirmed my ticket and beat a hasty retreat out of Africa, heading for the wintry climes of Great Britain. Trouble was, though I loved and missed my family, I really didn't want to go home. I yearned for a change. In retrospect, it's laughable that I'd spent most of December pining for the very things I said I didn't want, trying to recreate the very scenes I was apparently avoiding. Therapy, anyone?

I flew out of Tripoli without giving specific details to my mum and stayed near London, with Melanie, my best friend in Libya. I was burdened with self-reproach. The habit of gathering at Christmas is so entrenched that most of us can't imagine not going through with it. Naturally, I now accept that Christmas can be awful for other families, but it hadn't sunk in back then. I still insisted that every household but mine had meaningful celebrations filled with sweetness and light.

The morning after I arrived in the UK, I sat in a London cafe with a bunch of other expats on leave and heard the pop single

"Do They Know It's Christmas?" by charity supergroup Band Aid. As we listened to the song about third-world starvation, Melanie shoved a whole jam-filled doughnut in her mouth. She couldn't chew, her mouth was so full; there was sugar all over her lips and raspberry jam running down her chin. It was a joke and I laughed with everyone else, but I thought, *What am I doing here?* I mean, these were good people (even if they didn't catch the irony of Ethiopia's poverty v. the ability to eat a doughnut like John Belushi) and I *was* looking for a change. But this wasn't it, didn't feel right. My own family wasn't so very far away. No decision to be made, really; this was a no-brainer.

I stepped out of the café and crossed the street to one of those iconic English red phone boxes. Just standing in the stinky airless kiosk made me weepy, and I hadn't even picked up the receiver! Moments after I dialed, my cash clinked into the moneybox, and I heard Mum's dulcet tones: "Winchester 69861. This is Elizabeth." That was her standard answer in her (slightly exaggerated) posh telephone voice. My stiff upper lip betrayed me instantly, and my lower one, too, which wobbled precariously as my face crumpled and unbidden tears sprang to my eyes. I needed a deep breath before I could say, "Happy Christmas, Mum! I'm back. Catching the next train." It's supremely simple, y'all: in spite of myself, I wanted to be with people who loved me, or purported to love me, even if it was only because we were related.

As I walked up Elm Road from Winchester Railway Station and saw in the front window our little fake tree adorned with those acorn and fir cone ornaments we'd handmade as children, and twinkling with tiny white lights, my cynical heart's pilot light ignited. What is it about Christmas tree lights that bring one's heart to life? As I stepped into our snug home, my precious mother handed me a glass of sherry. "Welcome home, dear. I was a bit worried you weren't going to make it!" and I felt better. It might not have been perfect, but it was familiar, and there was comfort in that familiarity. Maybe—and not for the first time, I know, before you remind me—I recognized the sense that the celebration of Christmas was less about what was happening on the outside and much more about a particular feeling on the inside. It was just a glimmer, mind you. I don't want to get all Hallmarky on you. But it was there, like a seed, a germ of an idea, waiting for the spring of my maturity, which seemed never to emerge.

CHAPTER 10

Puss in Boots in North Africa

"After tea, they had some music. For they were a musical family, and knew what they were about, when they sung a Glee or Catch, I can assure you: especially Topper, who could growl away in the bass like a good one, and never swell the large veins in his forehead, or get red in the face over it. Scrooge's niece played well upon the harp; and played among other tunes a simple little air (a mere nothing: you might learn to whistle it in two minutes), which had been familiar to the child who fetched Scrooge from the boarding-school, as he had been reminded by the Ghost of Christmas Past."

Having shopped like a loon and filled up my suitcases both with food and new clothes, as was customary before returning for a tour of secretarial duty in Libya, I flew back on Saturday, 5th January 1985. Christmas had come to an end again, and as I sipped a G&T on the plane, I reflected—as I always did after the New Year parties were over and I'd recovered from my hangover—on whether I had enjoyed myself, on where Christmas 1984 registered on the magic-o-meter, the happiness scale I employed to decide such things.

Why, you may ask, was I so obsessed with "whether I had enjoyed myself"? I wish I could tell you precisely; I'm not 100 percent sure. I only know that the Holiday season and my feelings about it were all tied up with my peculiar family and whether I felt loved and included. What I considered to be "a good Christmas" could hold me emotionally for quite some time, months even, like an allergy shot. "At least I had a good Christmas!" might cross my mind when my January birthday turned out to be shite. "At least I had a fine time over the Holidays!" I might think when no Valentine card arrived. It looks ridiculous in writing and it may well be so, but there it is. My therapist earns her fee during Santa season.

But I digress. With my second G&T, I decided that Christmas on hiatus from Tripoli in our Winchester family home had turned out much the same as ever. I'd got home so late in December, I missed the joy of carol singing and the wonderful High Street bustle. Mum had offered to get tickets for the Christmas pantomime in the Odeon Southampton, but I left it too late to get organized. However, once I recovered from my regret that I hadn't had the gumption to remain in Tripoli, it was all about mingling with family and friends.

One thing that had changed drastically in recent years was Christmas dinner. Our mother had by this time given up meat altogether, so there was no turkey, chicken, or any other festive fowl. And she no longer used lard—that delectable, artery-clogging killer —so her roast potatoes didn't taste anywhere near as scrumptious. I missed that part of the conventional roast, even if it was giving me heart disease. Sis and I usually provided a couple of vegetarian quiches to liven things up a bit. Then we'd watch TV, slumped in armchairs like beached whales.

Another thing had shifted. Mum was preparing to retire from teaching and had taken on a part-time job as a Winchester City Guide. Her new favorite Christmas activity was walking downtown on Christmas Day, popping into the cathedral for a dose of spirituality, then picking up a bunch of senior American tourists from the Wessex Hotel and taking them on a tour. "Those crazy Americans," she'd say, "they've found the answer. Abandon the family, go to another country, and skip the whole kit cat and caboodle." (The phrase is "kit and caboodle" but ours always had a cat in it.) You'll notice, she only needed a small dose of spirituality. My mother's changes resonated with me. I was a bit offended by the idea of her abandoning us. However, the fact that she was doing, as Monty Python suggested, "something completely different" and that her tourists were accidentally encouraging her by example was fascinating. Incidentally, those Americans were great tippers—the English are crap at tipping, but they're excellent at hanging around Americans when it's tipping-time. When her guiding was over, they always wanted to take Mum for coffee or a drink. She'd go for coffee and schmooze with them—they *loved* schmoozing with Mum because she had that posh English accent, which she'd embellish, just to entertain. Mum tended to be timid but she was in her element on those tours, particularly with Americans. I watched her grow into the role of performer, something I never thought possible; she was quite the star of her own show, long before I was in the biz. Her wicked humor shone through, and she became amazingly adept at witty one-liners. Those zingers made her buckets of extra cash. Anyway, she'd finish her coffee, pocket her tips, and head off to her next stop, which could be the pub for a wee dram or straight home for a slap-up utterly un-Christmassy veggie banquet. That particular year, it was a "swift half," a.k.a. a Gold Label barley wine, at the South Western with Sis and me.

On New Year's Eve, my buddies and I ended up at the local rugby club for our drunken midnight festivities. In England, people often dress in costume for New Year's parties, but I'd nothing arranged so I went as my rather mixed-up self. At every tottering step of our pub crawl, I avoided old boyfriends—seriously, are you still counting?—who tended to frequent the same watering holes. As anyone who's ever lived in a small town will tell you, avoiding one's exes can be an ongoing problem.

Now that I thought about it, perhaps Christmas wasn't "the same as ever." And what happened next in Tripoli certainly threw a shiny new spanner in the works, one which was to influence my December schedule increasingly in years to come.

My friends and fellow secretaries, Melanie and Alison, who had also spent the Holidays with their families, met me at Tripoli airport, and in the car, we exchanged accounts of our respective English vacations and discussed what we'd brought back in our luggage.

The following morning at the office, we were regaled with stories of exciting activities in our absence: a visit via helicopter with a raucous bunch of Italian colleagues for Christmas dinner on an oil rig! What?! I couldn't believe I'd missed such an adventure. A day-trip to Leptis Magna at the New Year! Leptis Magna was a world-renowned Roman site that I'd been desperately hoping to visit since my arrival in Libya nearly a year earlier. Nooooooo! I fumed with envy. There had never been an opportunity to visit Leptis Magna before, and I knew it was a one-off that wouldn't happen again. I pictured myself at the stupid Winchester Rugby Club and I was profoundly peeved. *If only I'd hung around*, I thought, *what an idiot I was to run away!* Those who'd been patient and stayed the course had done the very thing I'd originally been trying so hard to do—they'd made the most of Christmas where they were.

I sank into a pitiful post-Christmas despondence, made all the worse by my friends' constant reminiscences of their escapades. And then something wonderful came my way that I barely knew existed: community theatre. The Tripoli Players, our local theatre group, was presenting "Puss in Boots," a traditional English panto-mime, and the panto was on Mum's Christmas list of *Things to Do*. I was being given a chance to salvage Christmas!

Ah, the panto! As a rule, Americans don't have pantos—it's terribly British. Theatres in cities and provincial towns through-out the UK still produce an annual professional pantomime in December/January. It's a popular form of family theatre with a long history, incorporating song, dance, buffoonery, slapstick, cross-dressing, in-jokes, topical references, audience participation, and mild *but essential* sexual innuendo, as only the Brits know how. Think Hans Christian Andersen meets Benny Hill with a cheeky bit of Eddie Izzard thrown in for good measure.

All right, I'll acknowledge that the Tripoli Players' "Puss in Boots" didn't take place until after I got back from my UK visit. I can practically hear you protesting: "This has nothing to do with Christmas!" But if you've been following at all, you'll appreciate its significance. Instead of wallowing in defeat, I dragged my sorry arse out of my comfort zone and into something practical . . . *(cue amateur dramatic thespian tones)* THE THEATRE!

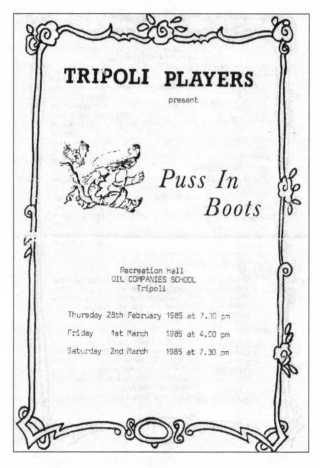

TRIPOLI PLAYERS

present

Puss In Boots

Recreation Hall
OIL COMPANIES SCHOOL
Tripoli

Thursday 28th February 1985 at 7.30 pm

Friday   1st March   1985 at 4.00 pm

Saturday 2nd March   1985 at 7.30 pm

(It should be noted that, while invited to audition, I declined, being too fearful to take the stage, despite lofty dreams. I'm in the program under "Make-up/Hair" because my confidence only went so far. Ironically, all my theatre colleagues will confirm that my talents at "Make-up/Hair" are laughable, even after a lengthy stage career. If no one's available to take on the styling of this ham-fisted performer's hair, the phrase generally bandied about by costumiers is "Get her a wig!")

28 February 1985
Dear Mum,

It's the Tripoli Players panto this weekend. The first performance is tonight, and if yesterday's dress rehearsal is anything to go by, they may as well leave the country right now. It was appalling. No one knew their lines and two of the principal characters didn't even turn up. On a personal note, I've been messed around right from the start, and was absolutely furious to find that, although a great deal of fuss was made about my being "make-up coordinator," I was actually considered "junior helper" and treated as such. For a start, no one told me that our dress rehearsal commenced at 6:00 PM so I duly arrived at 7:30 PM (the usual time) to find that all the hair/make-up had already been done by a nice Malaysian lady who (I had been told) was to be my assistant. Anyhow, I've now handed the reins to my Malaysian friend, and have accepted my role as her helper. Tomorrow is the matinee performance—I found this out two nights ago! But Saturday will be the best night because all my expat friends are going to the show, and all the Tripoli Players who are not acting will be there to watch, including me. The last night is always good! [I write, as if I have a clue] I just pray that the cast pull themselves together on the night! Melanie is cooking lasagna for us, and I'm bringing the remainder of a shepherd's pie. It's all terribly exciting!

So there you have it. With a smidgeon of lucky timing and a wee bit of courage, I managed to (a) get involved in my first Christmas production since primary school, (b) experience an unexpectedly cool Holiday event, and (c) rescue Christmas.

All hail the gods (and goddesses) of sulky dyspeptic secretaries! *Bows deeply.*

CHAPTER 11

Christmas and the Working Girl

"Oh! But he was a tight-fisted hand at the grindstone, Scrooge! a squeezing, wrenching, grasping, scraping, clutching, covetous old sinner! Hard and sharp as flint, from which no steel had ever struck out generous fire; secret, and self-contained, and solitary as an oyster. The cold within him froze his old features, nipped his pointed nose, shrivelled his cheek, stiffened his gait; made his eyes red, his thin lips blue; and spoke out shrewdly in his grating voice. A frosty rime was on his head, and on his eyebrows, and his wiry chin. He carried his own low temperature always about with him; he iced his office in the dog-days; and didn't thaw it one degree at Christmas."

In 1987, I was employed at the Jebel Ali Hotel*, one of the first beach resort hotels in Dubai, before Dubai became the Manhattan of the Middle East, or at the very least, of the United Arab Emirates. The hotel is just off the main road between the emirates of Dubai and Abu Dhabi, known in my day as the Dubai-Abu Dhabi Road or Sheikh (pronounced "shake" and not "sheek") Zayed Road, both of which conjure up in my mind wistful images of deserts, camels, and all things Arabian. It's been demystified now and is called E-11. Way to go, Dubai.

The original Jebel Ali Hotel opened in 1981, years before the Jebel Ali Free Zone and the still incomplete Palm Jebel Ali, between which it is wedged today. It was there before Dubai Investment Park, Jumeirah Golf Estates, and Legoland Dubai. It was, in those days, a single hotel between sand and sea in the middle of nowhere.

The Jebel Ali Free Zone (Jafza) was still a work in progress; Palm Jebel Ali wasn't even a twinkle in a local businessman's eye.

From a distance, the Jebel Ali, as we affectionately referred to it, was like a mirage, shimmering in a haze of pale yellow, almost white sand that merely hinted at the Persian Gulf beyond. If you ever dreamed of caravan trails and spice roads and Arabian Nights, this faraway paradise might have played a role in your make-believe. The first time I saw it, I was entranced—a magical castle, a fantastical, almost fanciful image in the heat and wind. The closer we got, driving alongside aimless wandering camels, on tarmacked winding roads across desert scrub, and the more the mirage took shape, the deeper in love I fell with that white palace, and the more enamored I became at the very idea of my being a part of its majesty. How lucky I was! What a dream come true for this shy twit from England. Forget Libya, this was it. This was my fantasy job becoming a reality.

I wasn't pleased to discover that I had to work on Christmas Day. My contract apparently stated that I was an essential worker, and that year, contrary as ever, I *wanted* to go home for Christmas. Although my employment papers stated clearly that it would be impossible, I had inquired generally about the possibilities of a December vacation. The general manager*, or "The Boss" as he was generally known, for whom I worked as secretary/assistant, scoffed visibly, almost disbelieving, when I brought it up in casual conversion. "Are you joking? It is one of our busiest times. You know it's out of the question. I can't imagine what you're thinking." He shook his head and laughed. And that was that.

I was wretched that first Dubai December*. The hotel had turned out to be nothing like I'd expected. Like most mirages, it was an illusion. The hotel's purpose was to create illusions, and my fantasy job was one of them. The post for which I'd applied seemed radically different from the impression I'd received at the interview in London. Like employees the world over, I was overworked, underappreciated, and underpaid. More significantly, I believed I was the wrong person for the position, being more introvert than extrovert, and unused to being given orders as if I were a child. I also felt inadequate, trailing in the footsteps of the most efficient secretary in the history of office management, who'd been there since before construction, whose very name brought respect and fear to management and workers alike. My coaching and handover took three hard months, and it wasn't enough. Three months almost to the day, my predecessor abandoned me to my fate. After seven years, she wasn't going to stay a day longer than she had to. I wanted to hang on to her ankles to stop her physically from walking into the red, sandy sunset; I wanted to scream, "Don't forsake me!" but when Christmas arrived, I was alone. Like a selkie unable to return to her sea-home because her clothes have been stolen, I became, once more, a fish out of water.

On the subject of illusions, you should know that, unlike Libya, the *conventional* Victorian Christmas was alive and well in Dubai, celebrated in hotels such as the Jebel Ali; and while most European Christian expats living on the banks of the Persian Gulf observed the season in their flats or villas, many took advantage of holiday merriment at their favorite hotel.

I would suggest that, most of the time, we've no notion of who's working on our behalf over Christmas. I'm editing this piece during the early days of the COVID-19 pandemic, when new respect is being shown to the frontline workers, i.e., the noble folk, who hold down the fort when the general public is taking care of family, friends, and of course, themselves: shop workers, drivers, restaurateurs, waiters, cooks, cleaners, medical staff on call. In the case of the "coronavirus quarantine," it's a life-and-death situation, all day every day, whereas in usual circumstances, we're talking a few times a year on public holidays. All the same, I bet that it's normal practice to take for granted staff members slogging out their guts so you can have a good time.

The Jebel Ali Hotel was famous for its Christmas display. People came from all around the Persian Gulf just to behold it. Oh, how hard the staff worked to make it perfect for the guests! The lobby was, on an ordinary day, fabulously stunning, with golden elevator doors and sparkling tendril lighting; at Christmastime, it was splendiferous! There was a life-size replica of Santa's sleigh suspended precariously above the vast expanse of marble floor. There were Norwegian spruces with blinking lights surrounded by fake snow. Chef Lee and his patisserie team baked and built a gingerbread house just like the one I always pictured in Hansel and Gretel; children loved playing in it ("Can we eat it, mummy?"), and its scent permeated the entire place. I recollect carolers dressed in full Victorian costume singing about "the bleak mid-winter" with sweat dripping down their faces on to their woolen scarves and mittens . . . or did I dream that? At the same time, *outside* the hotel, through the back windows, you could see youngsters splashing about in the swimming pool, their parents sipping piña coladas with colorful umbrellas at the swim-up bar, half-naked sunbathers on loungers coating themselves with Coppertone while palm trees swayed in the warm breezes of the Arabian sea. Every now and then, the two worlds would collide as sunburned, sand-coated children with plastic swim-rings around their middles and stripy towels around their necks wandered through the snow-covered lobby to get roasted chestnuts. Or as red-suited Santa himself—the English sales manager, as I recall—sack in hand, sweat streaming down his face, walked across the beach volleyball courts calling "Ho-ho-ho!"

*The gingerbread house near the windows
overlooking the pool*

I've often wondered: did anyone catch the irony that Jesus was more likely born in the simple sandy world outside the window, with the heat and the date palms, than he was in the air-conditioned indoor world of hot chocolate, roaring fires, and ornamented fir trees?

Throughout December, I took my now tear-stained copy of Charles Dickens' *A Christmas Carol* and read it at lunchtime while trying to relax on the hotel's private beach—and sitting rather absurdly in full secretarial garb among the swim-suited German holiday-makers. I was stoic and tried not to let it bother me, but when I was overwhelmed by thoughts that I'd made another huge career mistake, or missed my family, which was often in those days, I shed a few self-indulgent tears before pulling myself together. Life goes on, right?

Life did go on, relentlessly. In fact, life was pissing me off. And the part of it that was really getting to me was this whole *working on Christmas Day* business. Boy, I resented that. It wasn't the Boss who became Scrooge in this scenario; it was I. I transformed into a "squeezing, wrenching, grasping, scraping, clutching, covetous old sinner" myself, especially when I discovered that, though the hotel

85

was packed with international tourists, Dubai expatriates, and personal friends who did get the day off, there was absolutely no reason for me to be in my office. Nothing needed to be done in my office that day. Oh, I could have done some typing or caught up on filing, but the phone didn't ring, no one visited, nothing had to be done that couldn't wait until the next day. The Boss, always the socialite, barely stepped into his office. He worked his way around the hotel and networked like the professional he was, nurturing guests, sitting with different family groups at breakfast, lunch, and dinner, making sure everyone was thriving, and putting out fires only when necessary. I wanted to slap the congenial smile from his affable face. He was a fine representation of the homegrown hospitality that was the hotel's mission—and I never disliked him more.

He wanted me to be the same, encouraging me to chit-chat with visitors, but I didn't have it in me at the time; the inhibition that had often been an issue made social interacting a struggle. I recognize now that my duties on that Christmas Day were undemanding, certainly compared with the rest of the staff, who were on serious overload, and it wouldn't have been fair for me to get a day off. That didn't occur to me until later, more's the pity. I paced around the lobby, scowling at folks enjoying their Christmas day, whinging under my breath about my hard luck. "Humbug!" I mumbled to no one in particular, "Humbug!"

For me, the highlight of that particular Christmas Day at the hotel was the holy mass arranged for the Catholic workers, indeed any Catholics who wanted to attend. I went along, despite having lost my Catholicism by this time, because I was desperate for an injection of genuine seasonal spirit. The use of one of the small banqueting rooms had been approved by the Boss and thereafter lovingly decorated by the Catholic workers. Oh, what a brilliant sight it was! Barely an inch of the room wasn't adorned with brightly-colored flashing lights. If there's one thing I learned about folks from India eastwards, it's that they love color and if they can make it flash in any way at all, they will. Europeans can be so dull in contrast, and the less said about the British, the better.

A table was set up as an altar. On it was a white tablecloth, candles, and a small, decorated Christmas tree; all around it were electric twinkling lights. To the side of the altar, there was a crèche with Mary, Joseph, the Baby Jesus, shepherds, sheep, cattle, donkeys, and of course the Wise Men . . . they were all there. This delightful biblical birth scene pulsed with little lights like a radioactive bomb about to go off. If the Wise Men had lost their way, they would've found it easily. No guiding star required at the Jebel Ali Hotel!

I managed to hold back my gnawing desire to laugh because I didn't want to hurt anyone's feelings, but at the precise moment the priest held up the chalice, the Baby Jesus somehow arranged it so that all the flashing lights fell into sequence and began to throb at the same time. It was like the jackpot had been won simultaneously on all the one-armed bandits at the Bellagio Las Vegas. I totally lost it, along with the contents of my nose. I had to race out of the room, pretending I had a nosebleed. It was the most stimulating part of what was otherwise a dismal Christmas Day.

Humbug, I say, humbug!

See Appendices

CHAPTER 12

An Arabian Christmas

"'Why, it's Ali Baba!' Scrooge exclaimed in ecstasy. 'It's dear old honest Ali Baba! Yes, yes, I know! One Christmas time, when yonder solitary child was left here all alone, he did come, for the first time, just like that. Poor boy! And Valentine,' said Scrooge, 'and his wild brother, Orson; there they go! And what's his name, who was put down in his drawers, asleep, at the Gate of Damascus; don't you see him! And the Sultan's Groom turned upside-down by the Genii; there he is upon his head! Serve him right. I'm glad of it. What business had he to be married to the Princess!'"

W hen I left the Jebel Ali in May 1989 for a higher-paid position closer to downtown Dubai, the Boss, operating in what I now recognize as paternal mode, took me aside and warned me about the American businessman I'd chosen to work for. I felt he was sour grape-ing my decision, and I was desperate enough to leave the hotel to disregard his counsel outright. Alas, my new employer lived up to the warnings, and once there was no turning back (contract signed, visa transferred, etc.), I learned from others of his dire reputation, and knew I'd made a dreadful mistake. As a result, most of my time at this second job was spent trying to find another!

Boss #2 was an eccentric, irrational, and difficult man in his fifties. He was also exceedingly wealthy and owned a trading company, which we'll call The Trading Company. Every day, he went home for lunch at noon, saying he'd be back at 3:00 p.m. At first, I believed him and expected him, but it soon became clear that he was never going to return after lunch. In eighteen months, he did so only once. Well, he could do as he pleased, right? He'd phone at some point during the afternoon to give instructions or dictate letters to be completed before I left at 6:00 p.m. Those calls were weird and his instructions even weirder, e.g., to send spiteful recriminatory notes to his friends, to order bizarre products for his merchandise list, to have me reorganize his office. The following morning, he'd never recall these commands and would accuse me of rebelliousness and dishonesty. Occasionally, his requests were so odd, I hesitated before fulfilling them, choosing to check with him first. Whenever I didn't carry out his orders, he'd scold me for incompetence, then reproach me for my arrogant defiance, blaming the latter on my Britishness. I later discovered that he drank several Manhattans before lunch and a bottle of wine during lunch, then slept until he woke. He'd call me while still drunk, which explained the perverse instructions. And, every morning, he was horribly hungover, which explained his being a miserable git. Eventually, eighteen months later, I found job #3, and at the end of my final day, the miserable git returned to the office for the one and only time. I was packing my property into a scrappy old product box that I'd found in the trash, when he thundered in, dangerously plastered. He accused me of stealing the cardboard box. "It's my box," he slurred. "I own it. Empty it and give it me." With my heart hammering and hands shaking, I removed my stuff as quickly as I could and handed him the box. I left the office with my head held as high as I could manage, my possessions clutched awkwardly to my chest. He leaned against the doorframe, watching as I hobbled towards the elevator. "And may God forgive you for your wicked soul" were the last words I heard, as the lift door closed*.

While neither the job at the hotel nor The Trading Company worked out, each in its way helped me develop upper-level management skills, grow in maturity, and learn how to stand up for myself. It wasn't until the third job—a post with an irrigation-landscaping company near the Dubai Trade Centre (the tallest building in the

Middle East at the time)—that I developed a settled feeling and along with it, a sense of contentment.

With the introduction of office computers, I learned new talents (WordStar, WordPerfect, Lotus 1-2-3) and my resume expanded exponentially. However, my daily labor was in itself dull, being secretarial in nature—shorthand and audio typing, minute-taking, report-making, bookkeeping, never-ending piles of filing, with office management tossed in just for fun. Contact with the outside world during an average work day was rare. I knew my overactive brain and burgeoning self-confidence wouldn't allow me to function under such circumstances forever, but for the most part, I liked my coworkers and *(blast of trumpet fanfare here)* I no longer felt overworked, underpaid, and under-appreciated. That's no small thing.

During my three-month probation period, I wasn't provided with the housing that was included in my employment contract, so I spent the 1990 Christmas season, age thirty-three, sharing a tiny apartment with a woman who called herself a friend and her nutty dog, Derek. Derek ate the Christmas tree; that's the kind of nutty I'm talking about. And he pooped it too.

On Christmas Day itself, however, something marvelous happened. Most expat singles and young childless couples in Dubai celebrated the actual day with their friends in apartments or villas, and that year, I was invited to a gathering held in an authentic Middle Eastern house with a large, central, stone-paved courtyard sheltered by willowy palm trees. All the rooms, including the kitchen, went off the central courtyard. In the corners sat enormous pots with Ficus trees and bright pink bougainvillea plants, still blooming in December and growing up the inside walls, their trunks so thick you could see how old the original plants were.

It was a typically warm December, so a table had been set for twelve, outdoors in the courtyard. The Arab setting was so perfect you could almost picture Scheherazade and the Sultan sitting down to partake in a spectacular feast with marvelous stories to follow. This image was slightly distorted by the Christmas crackers by each plate and the delicious aromas of the English turkey dinner that filled the air. Also somewhat incongruous was the twinkling, colorfully decorated fir tree in the corner of the yard, beside the bougainvillea. All the same, this was a beautiful blend of European expatriate and local Arab themes.

Waxing so poetic here, the day sounds purely reflective and sentimental. Not at all! Here's a party of single expats, predominantly Brits, without children to influence behavior or families to enforce traditions. Let the games begin! Martin, the host, sported a gaudy pink and purple Hawaiian shirt. His girlfriend, Angela, had fashioned a Christmas-tree dress, all green netting and tinsel, with a twelve-inch plastic angel on her head. Everyone else wore flamboyant beach outfits—there was no one to dictate otherwise. At thirty-five, Martin was the eldest there, and he set the standard. I wore black because I'm an idiot.

As guests arrived, drinks were served from the outdoor bar. It was only noon, but so what? The sun was over the yardarm somewhere in the world. Martin was in his element, grabbing bottles and waving them in the air. "Okay, old chums! We've enough booze here to float the flippin' *Titanic*. Crazy cocktail, anyone? No holds barred. Whatever you like!"

"Got any gin?" I asked. "I'd love a real martini, a *gin* martini, shaken not stirred, three olives." Next thing you know, I'm sipping an ice-cold martini, and others are glugging and grimacing at whatever alcoholic monstrosity has been placed in their eager paws.

Prior to the food (which smelled so delightful, my mouth was watering), the gift exchange took place. As I wasn't acquainted with all the attendees, I wasn't really involved in the present-opening, so I can be forgiven for my mild jealousy; but I didn't let it show, smiling throughout. Martin's best friend, Graham, yelled with elation as he unwrapped remote-controlled cars and accompanying track, which was set up right there and then, becoming the highlight of the party. Graham's girl, Sally, received roller skates, tied them on directly, and wore them all day, rattling around on the courtyard stone. There were books, black-market cassettes, and cartons of cigarettes. One lucky lady was given a gorgeous Arabian birdcage that I liked so much, I involuntarily cried, "Oh, wow!" and which I'd have nabbed if I could have! By the end of the rambunctious exchange, the ground was strewn with paper, and my eyes prickled with melancholy at the thought my own childhood gift-giving. And just like in my family, guests played with their new toys throughout the afternoon, proving that grown-ups everywhere revert to childhood once Santa has been to town. I couldn't help but get swept up in the occasion, throwing my head back with vicarious laughter; these folks knew how to have fun!

When the group sat down to a multicultural dinner of turkey, sage-and-onion stuffing, roast potatoes, and Brussels sprouts, combined with local vegetables, cous-cous, and Persian salads, I was moved by an almost overwhelming feeling of joy—of community and sharing and love. We probably looked daft, singing English Christmas carols, paper hats on our heads, while palm fronds rustled above us and the Islamic call to prayer blared out from the mosques, but that's when I reminded myself that I was closer to the actual birthplace of Jesus right here in this Arabian courtyard than I'd ever been in my life.

Boxes of Australian plonk—cheap, plentiful, and ubiquitous in the Dubai booze shops—fulfilled our wine requirements. We quickly demolished one, and as a fresh box was opened, Graham did his best Monty Python voice: "A lot of people in this country pooh-pooh Australian table wine." Then Martin picked up the baton, "This is a pity, as many fine Australian wines appeal not only to the Australian palate, but also to the cognoscenti of Great Britain . . ." and every guest, apparently familiar with Eric Idle's famous routine*, erupted with laughter.

By the time liqueurs were served, folks were pretty sozzled—I sure was—but booze still flowed, along with terrible jokes: "Why did the three wise men smell like smoke? Because they came from afar!" Scotch emerged as if from nowhere, and we felt obliged to test several varieties, as one does, just to ensure that it wasn't poisoned. And when Martin and Angela forced us to participate in party games, such as blind man's buff and pin the tail on the donkey, we proved that they're nigh impossible to play when blotto.

As the evening drew to a close, the remaining revelers sat around, hardly functioning, but still sharing anecdotes. I leaned my head back to look through the palms at the shimmering stars. I was too plastered to register much, though I was already warm with nostalgia, conscious that, as Christmases go, this one would be tough to beat. I think I slurred something unctuous like "I'm ever so grateful that you let me join your party." Looking back now, I'm still stirred by a wistful sense of wonder at the multicultural ambiance of the day: that English-Arabian table of plenty, the lighthearted merriment, those sincere moments of connection, a lasting feeling of being included in a home away from home. And the birdcage . . . I'll never forget the birdcage.

See Appendices

CHAPTER 13

Robin Hood: The Secret Behind the Tights

"There were more dances, and there were forfeits, and more dances, and there was cake, and there was negus, and there was a great piece of Cold Roast, and there was a great piece of Cold Boiled, and there were mince-pies, and plenty of beer. But the great effect of the evening came after the Roast and Boiled, when the fiddler (an artful dog, mind! The sort of man who knew his business better than you or I could have told it him!) struck up "Sir Roger de Coverley." Then old Fezziwig stood out to dance with Mrs. Fezziwig. Top couple too; with a good stiff piece of work cut out for them; three or four and twenty pair of partners; people who were not to be trifled with; people who would dance, and had no notion of walking."

Once the three-month probation period was up in February 1991, a series of perks came with my new position, and at the tippy-top of the list was a charming furnished apartment in the up-and-coming Dubai neighborhood of Satwa, just off Al Diyafah Street (which we called Satwa High Street), quite close to the now famous Jumeirah Beach. The apartment building was named Al Tariff Building and was variously known, for obvious reasons, as "the Pizza Inn Building" or "the building the Kitchen Restaurant is in," which helped me describe where I now lived. Expatriates found local names taxing and gave pretty much everything a nickname; it was the same in Libya. With this apartment move, I became a "Satwa Sally"—a single expatriate female living alone and supporting myself. A woman married to an expat—by definition non-working, due to visa rules—and living in Jumeirah was referred to as a "Jumeirah Jane."

I loved my new home, and when yuletide rolled around again, I loved it even more. This wasn't because I'd suddenly decided that I loved Christmas—that remained a struggle—but because the apartment was a refuge I could choose to decorate or not, depending on how I felt when the time approached. It was the first really nice place I'd occupied since arriving in 1987. I didn't know then that Christmas 1991 would be my last in the Persian Gulf.

As it happens, I did decorate that year. Unlike Tripoli, where I couldn't find a tree for love nor money, in Dubai they were available both in stores and from departing expats. I've no notion of where I acquired mine, nor where I got the baubles and lights, but a tree was set up, and right next to it, a drinks table. When we were small, Mum always kept sherry in the house, but in December, she splurged with other beverages. Her favorite, which I recall seeing on the Christmas display, was Dubonnet (a popular Sixties drink) served with Schweppes Bitter Lemon. I don't know of anyone who requests it now, but Sis and I certainly did in our experimental drinking days; it was the only alcohol we knew by name! At a later date, Gordon's gin was added to Mum's lineup, along with Roses Lime Cordial and Britvic Orange for mixing: "I'll have a gin and lime!" or "A gin and orange, please!" were words that became familiar.

(After we kids left home, Mum adopted a new tipple: a night-time martini, or, as she called it, "a ruin" because it was basically a tumbler of gin—no ice, of course, English people don't like ice in their drinks—with an extra dry vermouth bottle waved over the top of the glass. It was the same-style martini as was drunk by Noël Coward, who famously declared, "A perfect martini should be made by filling a glass with gin, then waving it in the general direction of Italy.")

Now, when I see a photo of my decorated flat, I'm stunned by the quantity of booze on my own drinks table. Was it all for Christmas, or did I always stock my bar so well? I don't even like most of the stuff I had to offer. I personally never held a Christmas shindig in my flat. I'd had dinner parties and social events, but I never hosted that special turkey dinner. I still wanted to be entertained by OPFs (other people's families). My place was never the right place.

Just before starting this third Dubai job, a godsend of huge magnitude came into my life, and not a moment too soon. While making adjustments in my work life, I also needed diverting from an all-encompassing social world. You see, in my search for things-to-do-to-stop-me-thinking-about-my-life, I had found the distraction of pubs, parties, nightclubs, and balls. Gathering to partake of a few bevvies after a long, stressful day at the office was *de rigueur* for expats and, despite my efforts to do otherwise, I fell into the wormhole. Self-medication was simply part of the life-style. Consequently, when I was invited to join the Dubai Drama Group, it was a blessing in easily recognizable disguise.

At first, I didn't participate in the Dubai Drama Group productions, just the socials, which didn't involve any talent other than the ability to drink booze, at which I excelled because, outside of my various office environments, that's what I did most. Drowning my sorrows had become a hobby.

All that changed in November 1991 when this predominantly English theatre company began preparing for its annual Christmas production: *Robin Hood*, a pantomime. Remember the panto, the Veddy British Entertainment I'd been involved in Tripoli? If you recall, they're popular with amateur dramatic societies, and the Dubai Drama Group was nothing if not an AMDRAM.

At the auditions for *Robin Hood*—or as one witty cast member called it, *Robin Hood: The Secret Behind the Tights*—it was suggested I try out for the lead role, that of Robin Hood himself (don't forget, the leading man in a panto is always a woman). "What? Me? No way!" I reckoned they were mad even to ask. Secretly, I had a desire to be Maid Marian, but when I read the script, I noticed she had a solo song. I could carry a tune in bucket, but honestly, the bucket was probably the best place for it. "I'd like a small role, a teeny weeny one," I said, "just not the back-end of a panto cow."

I was cast as Derek—a Merry Man—a small "but significant" role, I was told. "As long as I get to frolic about in green tights and jaunty jerkin," I said, "I'll be happy!" That was an understatement. I was friggin' over the moon! I could hardly believe it was happening. My dream of becoming an actress was suddenly coming true.

"Derek, the Merry Man" had ten proper lines, and in one scene, six words, all of which were "Well?" I was in all the Sherwood Forest scenes; that is to say, I'd be in full view of the audience for much of the play. I was surprised to discover, in early rehearsals, how difficult it is to be in character on stage when you have nothing to say. I tended to face the auditorium with my arms limp at my side, an insipid smile on my silly face, like a third grader. I've since coached elementary children in drama workshops, so I've witnessed it myself, but I wasn't aware of my own proclivity until our director pointed it out.

"Berni, please stop gawping at the audience," she said. "You look like a Gumby* and it's distracting."

So I gawped at her instead . . . like a Gumby.

"Erm . . ." I said, eloquently.

"Just stay involved with what's happening to Robin Hood and the other Merry Men. Focus on the action on stage."

That advice did help, and to further my process, I practiced at home, cultivating facial expressions: surprise, sadness, horror, disappointment, as I imagined *professionals* would do it. Yeah, I know; cut me some slack. This was unfamiliar territory to me, and I was just so chuffed. I talked to myself in mirrors—"I'm an AC—TOR!"—mugging like a loony. I'd been training my overactive face since infancy; this was my big chance! By the time I'd finished, I could've written the book on "How not to Stand Around like a Gumby."

I loved rehearsals, both on stage and backstage, even when my inexperience caused waves of inhibition. I loved the camaraderie, too; if I ever felt left out, it was doubtless my own propensity for introversion that caused it. Cast members brought snacks to the dressing room: sandwiches, cookies, and occasionally mince pies and Christmas cake, adding seasonal flavor to the show. The entire adventure was more exciting than anything that had happened to me in a long time, anything pleasant, that is. At last, I had something to look forward to during the day, something to write home about—literally, my letters to family in England were full of every thrilling detail. It was years since I'd anticipated something with such eagerness. Rehearsals were so absorbing I was barely aware that they were keeping me out of the pub, that I wasn't drinking. The sheer exhilaration of my evenings provided so much natural adrenaline that, when I got home, I didn't pour myself a glass of wine because I didn't want or need it. Regrettably, thirty years later, that's changed!

Just when I figured I'd got the whole thing down—when I was morphing into the next Meryl Streep—the panto team threw me a curve ball: a dance number with lots of thigh-slapping and stepping on and off logs, all to the tune of the Gary Glitter* hit, "I'm the Leader of the Gang" ("Do you wanna be in my gang, my gang, my gang; d'ya wanna be in my gang, oh yeah!"). The rest of my cronies were taking it in their stride. I was slack-jawed with bewilderment. Talk about lulling me into a false sense of security.

Look, I can dance, people. I got rhythm, baby. Oh, yes, I can bust a move as well as the next pert white English chick. If you haven't seen my Michael Jackson impersonation, you haven't lived. But I gotta be honest, I hadn't bargained for singing and dancing in front of an audience, at least not without having chugged a bottle of Beefeaters beforehand. Of course, I should've known, this being a panto 'n' all, that there would be a number for the Merry Men. Everyone else had a song; why wouldn't we? Moron.

I was thankfully well acquainted with the pop song in question—God knows, I'd strutted my teenage stuff to that ghastly ditty at some disco or other back in the 1970s—so that wasn't an issue. But the choreography and dance rehearsals were another matter. WTF?! My brain had never been trained to memorize a dance routine, not since school, anyway, not since Sis and I had gone to disco dancing classes after seeing *Saturday Night Fever*: "Up with the arm, point those fingers!" I was physically pretty fit, but not gifted in the *learning* of the dance; my current theatre colleagues are doubtless nodding and mumbling, "You still aren't, missy."

Now I dreaded evenings. During the day, I was snappy with coworkers and forgot what I was saying halfway through a sentence. When I thought about rehearsals, my hands got so shaky and sweaty, typing became an issue. "What the hell are you doing?" said Boss #3, catching me mid-thigh-slap when I should have been working on Sheikh Mohamed's accounts. No amount of private prep seemed to help, and it was little comfort that my cohorts were messing up as much as I. Seriously, when "Do you wanna be in my gang" boomed from the rehearsal cassette player, a less Glittery, more rubbish gang of Merry Men you wouldn't want to meet.

By dress rehearsal, most of Robin's happy crew had mastered the routine, while I *still* hadn't quite got to grips with it, in spite of extra practice. I was fine at home—I was Ginger Rogers in my living room —but on stage, not so much. An added problem was that I don't always focus well when I'm nervous, so while I was faffing about with my shoelaces, as if they had anything to do with my incompetency, a new instruction was given about where to make our first entrance. I didn't hear it. I looked from cast member to cast member; everyone was nodding so they'd obviously got it. I was too embarrassed to ask them to repeat it because I couldn't bear to be the only one not getting it—*again*! As I walked to my car, tears began to stream. I wished my mother were there to comfort me, but I had no one but myself, and I wasn't being especially cooperative: I wanted to punch myself in the face for my lack of focus, and box my own ears for my lack of confidence—that wasn't going to help anyone. So, when I reached my car, I climbed in, locked the door, put my hands on the steering wheel and screamed at the top of my voice.

In order to give us a decent preview performance prior to our opening night, the powers that be had made inquiries around Dubai to find us an audience. As a result, we had a full house made up of kids from the Aseef School* for special needs children. *They* got a free show; *we* got an appreciative test audience. And oh boy, were they ever appreciative! I'd like to say that they liked the show, but I couldn't state that for sure. They laughed at everything, *e-ve-ry-thing*, whether it was supposed to be funny or not. When they weren't laughing uproariously, they were shrieking with delight—at us? No idea! Maybe? And if they weren't laughing or shrieking, they were chattering with each other or with themselves. The one thing they were *not* is quiet. From our perspective, it was good practice, both for having people to watch us, and for raising our volume so that we could at least hear our fellow actors. I will say this though: those children openly . . . *unaffectedly* . . . enjoyed themselves. It's just not clear whether we had anything to do with it.

Opening night was more frightening for me than having a machine gun held to my head or hiding from the Libyan Morality Police. I didn't dare eat; I'd already lost my lunch from both ends. I stared longingly at the exit and thought: "I could leave now. No one would miss me, my ten lines, my six 'wells.' I don't want to be an actress; I like being a secretary." Then I heard, "Places!" and broke into a cold sweat, a regular occurrence at theatres in years to come. I slipped into a kind of sickly trance. Then the lights went down, I took a deep breath, and I stepped forward along with the other Merry Men. I was completely blinded by the lights, as I had been at preview, only much worse. It didn't matter; I didn't want to see the audience anyway. Nonetheless, after a short while, faces began to emerge from the gloom. Frozen by stage fright, I couldn't pull up a single instruction. Nor could I hear anything—even my ears were scared. It's possible that I didn't say my lines. At the end of the scene, I somehow managed to exit the stage.

Our next scene was the song-and-dance number. "Please kill me now," I thought. Our log was set stage right, ready for us to pick up as we went on stage, but no one told me that, since preview, the log had been painted black. In the between-scene blackout, I couldn't see it. I learned right there and then that I'm totally night-blind. I somehow fell right over the log and onto my hands and knees. There was a lot of scrambling in the dark, during which I lost my sense of direction altogether. I kept reaching for the hand holes on the log, and it wasn't until I hit a wall that I realized the log had gone. As the lights went up for our scene, I was still messing about in the wings when I heard my stage gang begin the song: I'd missed an entrance in my first show! I ran to join the routine but was so discombobulated, I never quite got into rhythm. It was actor's nightmare, like being naked on stage or learning lines for the wrong show. I hated myself and I knew the audience hated me too. They were as quiet as church mice which, after the hilarity of the preview performance, was crushing. And it was all my fault. I just wanted to die.

The director's notes after the show went something like this:
1. Who fell over the log backstage and why?
2. Why were the Merry Men so miserable?

It did get better—well, it had to, didn't it? And on the second night, the auditorium was packed to the gills with friends and family, who laughed and applauded and yelled back at us, exactly as they're supposed to in panto-land. We relaxed into our roles as entertainers, and when I say that, I really mean that my fellow actors relaxed . . . and I calmed down a bit. I even managed to turn the tables on myself, swinging, like a true arty-farty, from utter misery at the end of one night to sheer euphoria by the end of the next.

Sadly, that was when the ad-libbing—normal in pantos— started, which was all very well for the seasoned theatre peeps, but mortifying for me. Every time an actor changed a line to get a laugh, even if it wasn't my cue, I'd freeze, mouth agape, transfixed with horror. My mind would go as blank as a chalkboard. Ad-libbing is a skill that actors learn over time; for a newbie such as I, nothing improvised or extra could be added once I was on stage. I never got used to it.

I didn't conquer the stage fright either, but it eased off once we mastered the dance, for which we got resounding cheers by closing night. Also by closing, I'd mastered a different way of delivering each of my "wells"—in fact, I'd added three more—and they were making people laugh. This made me truly happy! Word on the street was that *Robin Hood* was the group's "best panto ever," so I was proud to have been a part of it: my very first show.

That pantomime *became* Christmas for me. I spent Christmas Day with a group of friends who were now vying for the opportunity to host the annual roast dinner, and I enjoyed it, but the AMDRAM production was my Christmas. Being onstage, however terrifying, and making others joyful with humor, singing, and dancing was the highlight of my year.

Until *Robin Hood*, I didn't realize I'd been looking for a seasonal activity to sink my teeth into. One can say "I want to *this* . . ." or "I want to *that* . . ." just as I always said, "I want to be an actor," but it doesn't amount to a hill of beans until you take a step in that direction. This was the start of something. I was taking a step in the right direction. And along the way, that step gave me one of the Merriest Christmases I'd ever had.

See Appendices

CHAPTER 14

A Tuna Christmas

"'I am the Ghost of Christmas Present,' said the Spirit. 'Look upon me!' Scrooge reverently did so. It was clothed in one simple deep green robe, or mantle, bordered with white fur. This garment hung so loosely on the figure, that its capacious breast was bare, as if disdaining to be warded or concealed by any artifice. Its feet, observable beneath the ample folds of the garment, were also bare; and on its head it wore no other covering than a holly wreath set here and there with shining icicles. Its dark brown curls were long and free: free as its genial face, its sparkling eye, its open hand, its cheery voice, its unconstrained demeanour, and its joyful air. Girded round its middle was an antique scabbard; but no sword was in it, and the ancient sheath was eaten up with rust. 'You have never seen the like of me before!' exclaimed the Spirit."

There's a bumper sticker that reads, "I wasn't born in Texas but I got here as fast as I could!" That doesn't refer to me. I never planned to come to Texas. If you'd told me I was going to end up in Texas, I would've laughed and laughed and laughed. But I'd always wanted to visit America, the land of opportunity, the land of new beginnings. And after five long years in Dubai, where I'd become as boring as I was bored, my life needed a swift kick up the whatnot to get it moving again. I was thirty-five.

I came to Austin, state capital of Texas, to spend a week with the only person I knew in the US. You see, I was passing through on my way to Los Angeles to become a movie actress. Yes, I'd decided that the easiest way to combat shyness, lack of confidence, low self-esteem, and high anxiety was to go to Hollywood and spend time with the Beautiful People. Clever girl!

My friend, Beth, had gone to the University of Texas and, like many before her, loved Austin so much, she'd never left. Our mothers had been pen friends since the 1940s and with their encouragement we became pen pals, too. In the early 1980s, she backpacked through Europe and stayed with my family in England. She'd always said I could stay with her in return, and reminded me of this in our correspondence. The idea took root.

As I sat in the plane on that first flight to America, I realized how blasé I'd become. Nothing could surprise me anymore. After Winchester, Tripoli, and Dubai, I was culture-shock-proof. Sipping my delicious airplane G&T, I thought about what I'd done to get me to this point: sold my house, sold my car, sold the last of my loser boyfriends . . . no, I just left him—no one would've paid good money for him. I'd gathered my resources, bought a ticket, and here I was. Some friends thought me brave; some, stupid. Teetering on a tightrope between bravery and stupidity, I was finding the line between the two harder and harder to distinguish. Like a Cirque du Soleil performer, on one side I saw a bottomless pool of turquoise water; on the other, crocodiles. I tried not to think at all.

My plan to spend a week in Austin changed to a month, then six months. I didn't have much money and wasn't allowed to work, so while Beth went out of town on business, I took care of her household instead of paying rent. As her pets disliked the kennels, and boarding them when she traveled was expensive, it was an ideal arrangement for both of us.

It wasn't long after I arrived, in October 1992, that new friends began asking, "Where are you going for Thanksgiving?" This is when I learned that Thanksgiving is really another name for the first event of Christmas. In my childhood home, nothing began before we opened the first day on the Advent calendar. In the US, the outdoor decorations and lights went up the morning after Turkey Day in the last weeks of November.

Here I was again: the new kid in town. Starting over in the land of opportunity, reinventing myself in the land of new beginnings. Perversely, I found myself homesick for both England and Dubai almost as soon as I'd settled in and, with Christmas around the corner, the homesickness was somehow worse. As soon as that fish-out-of-water feeling hit, I ran through the list of Mum's *Things to Do* to get me in the mood.

"What about a nativity scene," I thought, "like the one I grew up with?" America, considering itself a Christian country more than anything else, and being, frankly, more Christian than I believed an entire country could be, (and being also rather scratchy on the subject) had crèches and crib scenes out the wazoo. They were set up everywhere from church lobbies to front porches, shop windows to garage forecourts: every variety, every style. Christians from every world nation had their own Baby Jesus and their own depiction of the nativity. As a child, I'd wondered why Jesus was white with brown hair and blue eyes when he was from the Middle East, but I'd never imagined Native American, Hispanic, Asian, or African Baby Jesuses. There were even puppy and kitten Baby Jesuses. They certainly made a mockery of the Nasons' wooden shed and tiny figurines—be it ever so humble, etc.

When it came to fashioning homemade ornaments for a Christmas tree, or indeed, making my own tree as I'd done in Libya, well, why would I? As far back as early November, stores were already stocked with festive items. The selection took my breath away. Shoppers snapped them up as if there were no tomorrow, and in no time at all, sparkly trees appeared in every window, house, and yard. OMG, people's yards! These were full of life-size objects, like some new-fangled, modern-day alternative to a crèche: inflated snowmen, snow-ladies, snow-babies, Santas, twinkling reindeer, and candy canes by the trillion. And lights, lights everywhere, all shapes, all colors; still lights, flashing lights, strobe lights. Entire neighborhoods became wonderlands, using enough electricity to drain the national grid.

Then came the holiday music, playing in stores, 24-7. Sob! And not what I called seasonal music either, because there was nothing spiritual about it. I mean, I wasn't especially religious back then, but where were the blessed carols? The only songs I heard were silly frivolous songs like "Little St. Nick," or sexy ones like "Santa Baby" and "I Saw Mommy Kissing Santa Claus." Santa Claus! What's with the American obsession with Santa Claus? Doesn't anyone know the story of St. Nicholas? Santa, St. Nick, Kris Kingle, Santy. Argh! Too many Santas!

There was even a shop called the Christmas Store, WHICH WAS OPEN ALL YEAR ROUND! Why, people, why?! What was the point of a year-round Christmas Store? It was ridiculous. It didn't make sense. When I heard about it, I went there by bus—actually, a bus and a long walk; Austin's public transport wasn't up to much in those days—then I stood outside, because I couldn't bring myself to go in. I looked in the window, shaking my head at the blatant excess. The concept seemed almost sinful. How much shiny stuff does a person need? But I had to see it with my own eyes. I kept thinking, "When did America embark on this journey of seasonal consumerism? When did the business of Christmas become just that . . . business?" My Austin buddies thought I was a killjoy, a spoilsport, but I didn't get it. I still don't get it.

If you want to take the time to read about it, you'll discover that good ol' well-intentioned Charles Dickens brought the celebration of Christmas back into fashion with his popular *Christmas Carol*. He was ably assisted by Queen Victoria and Prince Berty, who began many of the customs we follow today. Joining that jolly threesome is another couple of reprobates: Thomas Nast with his picture of tubby Santa in his red suit and Clement C. Moore with his poem "A Visit from St. Nicholas" ("'Twas the night before Christmas . . .").

December 25th was still three weeks away, and I was already overwhelmed. Total overload. Something had happened to me that had never happened before. I was screaming "Too much Christmas!"

Clinging to Mum's list, I decided that a pantomime would be the answer: something to participate in and laugh along with, something not too serious—Christmassy and un-Christmassy at the same time. I went on a desperate search for an Austin panto. Surely there was a panto. Somewhere a panto. But no one had heard of pantos.

What I did find was a show called *A Tuna Christmas* at the Paramount Theatre on Congress Avenue, near the Capitol. I had walked around the downtown area a few times, riding the bus (No. 1 Lamar) from Beth's house in north Austin. I had already "done the tour" of the Paramount Theatre, and I loved that historic building! I didn't know then that I would work there for three years in the development office, nor that I would perform as an actress in the State Theatre next door. I only knew that I wanted to witness something on that old-fashioned stage, and I'd read good things in the local rag, the *Austin Chronicle*, about this Joe Sears/Jaston Williams comedy.

Not yet aware of Austin's reputation for casual chic, I dressed in my theatre finery and took my nosebleed seat at a Sunday matinee. I'd like to report that I was as delighted as publicity assured me I would be, but that would be a lie. Certainly, my fellow audience members, all twelve hundred of them, were helpless with laughter, tears streaming. And it was a sight to behold, with its bright, colorful set, and those two remarkable actors, playing more than ten characters apiece, male and female. I was in awe of their speedy costume changes and incredible transformations. Wow, if I could ever be as good as they, wouldn't that be something! Unfortunately, and this is extremely important, bearing in mind that the show had a real plot, I could not catch a single word either of them was saying. Whole sentences, indeed whole paragraphs, were spoken without my understanding a thing. They were loud enough, projecting as good actors do; that wasn't the problem. It was the broad Texas accents.

At the intermission, the lady sitting next to me leaned over and said, in an accent almost as thick as Sears and Williams, "How're yew enjoyin' it?" We'd introduced ourselves at the start of the show and she was over the moon to discover that I was English, telling me all about her British ancestors who'd been in Texas for generations and where in the UK they were buried. I think she was anxious I should appreciate a bit of her culture, outside of Texas. "I'm sorry," I admitted, "but although they're talking English, I can't make sense of anything. I've no clue what's going on." She laughed long and hearty. "Yep, that'll be them accents! It's like that in small-town Texas. Wait 'til you meet folks in the Panhandle. You'll never git a thang!"

I didn't have time to ask her what she meant by "the Panhandle" before the lights went down for the second act. About halfway through, I miraculously caught the rhythm of their speech, and I began to "feel" the language. By the end, I was able to understand most of it. "What a shame," I thought, "I never really found out what it was all about."

On the No. 1 Lamar bus home, I reflected on how I'd missed the experience of my first Austin theatre visit. How disappointing! Then it occurred to me that I had no deeds to do, no promises to keep. For the first time in my adult life, I didn't have a job or any real commitments. I'd do something I'd never done before. I'd see the show again!

The next day, I purchased another ticket. At the following Thursday evening's show, I took my seat in the stalls, close to the front. This time sporting jeans and t-shirt like a real Austinite, I watched those brilliant performers in all their artistic glory, so close I could see their facial expressions and everything. I followed every word, and appreciated every nuance. I got it!

As a postscript, I took a job at the Paramount Theatre in 1994, and received (as a perk) complimentary seats for several subsequent runs of *A Tuna Christmas*. I've never stopped loving the show; it brings back heady memories of my early time in town. How I would love to watch the masters at work again! And to bring the anecdote full circle, and confirm what my *Tuna* companion was talking about all those years ago, I've performed many times in the Panhandle since then. . . and I still struggle to identify those immortal words: "Hidee! Hyeru?"

CHAPTER 15

A Very Plaid Christmas

"Scrooge had a very small fire, but the clerk's fire was so very much smaller that it looked like one coal. But he couldn't replenish it, for Scrooge kept the coal-box in his own room; and so surely as the clerk came in with the shovel, the master predicted that it would be necessary for them to part. Wherefore the clerk put on his white comforter, and tried to warm himself at the candle; in which effort, not being a man of a strong imagination, he failed."

One thing I did to prepare myself for My First Texas Christmas was buy a fresh copy of *A Christmas Carol* from Austin's own independent bookstore, BookPeople. As you know, children, if you've been keeping up, I had read Charles Dickens' "little book" while sitting on the roof of my office block in downtown Tripoli and on the sandy beaches of the Persian Gulf in Dubai. My dog-eared copy was too torn and tear-stained to see me through another year. At the bookstore, I picked up a Christmas treasury called, with good reason, *A Christmas Treasury*, and that was where I read these immortal words: "It is cold, wet, and foggy in England at Christmastime."

NO, IT ISN'T! In the—count them!—thirty Christmases I spent in England, I'll grant you a few of them were cold, a few were wet, and some were foggy, but only a couple of them were cold, wet, and foggy all at the same time. We had many gorgeous Christmases when I was growing up. We walked to early Christmas Mass on cold frosty mornings and on bright sunny mornings. Once, we awoke in the early hours, hoping to see Father Christmas and instead finding snow, which lasted only until we got to church, but snow! The one fairly consistent thing? The temperature. It's cold. I will admit that. It is frickin' freezing in England in December. As everyone wants yuletide to be! I've observed how hard it is to cope with warm weather when you're trying to create a Dickensian Christmas.

There's only one other place I've lived where the weather on Christmas Day is as varied and unpredictable as my home in England . . . the same place where they say, "If you don't like the weather, wait ten minutes." Yep. Texas. Specifically, Central Texas. Will Rogers apparently coined that phrase about his home state, Oklahoma, but I'm claiming it for the Lone Star State for this story.

From my personal experience, Christmas Day in Central Texas can be literally anything from below freezing and icy to 90 degrees Fahrenheit and balmy. I'm not joking. You can be in snow-suit and snow boots or shorts and t-shirt. Also, the day can begin like the Arctic and end like equatorial Africa. Or the other way around, if a blue norther happens to pass through.

The term "blue norther" is pure Texas, or so the locals tell me. It's a weather phenomenon—a rapidly moving autumnal cold front that causes temperatures to drop really fast (as much as 30 degrees in a matter of minutes) and often brings freezing rain or snow, followed by blue skies and cold weather. My sources (the internet) advise that blue northers get their start when a bitterly cold air mass builds up not far from the North Pole. I won't go into the technical details (because I haven't got a clue) but suffice to say, when everything comes together, a cold front is produced that can race south at speeds of thirty-five miles an hour or more, enough to move it from Canada to the Gulf of Mexico in less than two days. The storm arrives with screaming winds that can push up a thick, ominous blanket of clouds. These may look blueish-grey as they approach; hence the colorful name. Or maybe it's because the weather gets so cold, everyone turns blue. What do I know?

I understand that the dramatic effects of the blue norther have been recorded and exaggerated since Spanish times in Texas, but I can tell you from sorry experience that this particular type of cold front can be pretty dramatic.

After extending my Texas visit, I'd made friends with a charming group of Austinites. One of them (let's call her Katy) had welcomed me to Thanksgiving dinner with her family in North Austin. As Christmas approached, I was again invited to spend the day with them. Apparently, I hadn't disgraced myself too horribly at the Thanksgiving football game by getting lost on the way back from the restrooms just as the game ended and seventy-five thousand people filed out of Texas Memorial Stadium.

My first Christmas Day in America, I awoke and prepared myself to be collected for a day of Holiday Fun with Katy's family. Beth was with her clan in Houston so, before I left, I fed her dog, Charlotte, and her four cats. It was unseasonably warm and humid and I dressed accordingly. The weatherman said a blue norther would sweep through the area later in the day, so I grabbed a cardigan, just in case.

On Christmas Eve, I'd started a slight cold. On Christmas morning, it was marginally worse with a headache, a cough, and a slightly woozy feeling. "No worries," I thought as I headed for Katy's waiting car. "I can live with a cold. I only hope I don't give it to anyone else."

Katy's family home was decorated for Christmas, Texas-style. And by this, I mean, BIG. If decorations in the US were on the extravagant side, those in Texas were BIGGER. In fact, everything in Texas was inclined to be the BIGGEST. This being my first personal encounter with such ornamentation, I was gob-smacked at the sheer quantity, from the fully festooned tree and monster inflated snowman (which was wheezing creepily with the aid of an electric airpump) in the front yard to the lights strung over practically every inch of the front of the house. If you've seen *National Lampoon's Christmas Vacation*, you'll have the image.

Inside the house was the same. There didn't seem to be a square inch that wasn't embellished. Other than at the Jebel Ali Hotel, I'd become accustomed to simpler times, shared with friends; this was the opposite end of the spectrum. Oh, and there was something else worth mentioning. Everything was adorned with plaid . . . big, bold plaid. Red and green plaid, I might perhaps have understood, but this was purple and blue. "Are you Scottish?" I asked, because a family tartan was the only reason I could imagine for someone to dress a house like a giant kilt. "Nope," said Katy with pride. "We're German!" She just liked plaid, and purple was her favorite color. The tree was covered with tartan bows; even in the bathroom, there was a tartan garland on the window ledge and a plaid outfit on the spare toilet roll. Frankly, it was all rather overwhelming and made me quite lightheaded; if I hadn't already been a bit under the weather, I might have developed something right then and there.

A line of festive stockings hung from the mantelpiece. I was moved almost to tears when I spotted one with my name on it. Despite its being warm and sultry outside, a massive log fire roared in the hearth, and everyone except me was sporting some sort of thick woolen sweater decorated with gingerbread men or candy canes or elves. Just looking at them made me hot. As a matter of fact, beads of perspiration appeared on my forehead. I became aware that my body was scorching, sweating copiously, and yet, at the same time, I was shivering from head to foot. I was suddenly so dizzy I was afraid I'd faint. Katy noticed and said, "Are you all right?"

I had to be honest. "No," I said, "I don't feel well at all."

Katy's mother took my arm to support me. "You've gone as white as a sheet," she said.

The smell of the food which had seemed so pleasant when I came in, was now nauseating. I felt horribly ill, and it wasn't the plaid. I realized too late that this wasn't a cold; it was more likely flu.

At my request, Katy immediately drove me home. Her family was sorry for me, but a large crowd was expected at this gathering, several of them elderly, and young children, too. There was a Christmas Day to celebrate, and they didn't want to expose their vulnerable folk to flu any more than I did.

Looking from the car window on the drive home, I noticed the sky darkening, a blue-grey line of thick bosomy clouds heralding the arrival of the blue norther. "That's what it's like inside my head," I thought.

Katy saw me into the house, adjusted the thermostat so that the heating would switch on when the temperature dropped, then left to return to her party. By this time, I didn't really care much about Christmas. I just wanted to lie down. Charlotte and the cats watched with detached interest as I clambered onto my double bed with all my clothes on and pulled up the covers.

At some point during the afternoon, I fed the animals, changed into my sweats and took my temperature. It was 102 degrees; my personal normal was 97. I got back into bed. I stared at the ceiling. "Should I call someone?" I mused vaguely. Everything was blurry now. As sickness took over, the winds of the cold front picked up, and the heating clicked on. There was a windchime outside my window that pealed like church bells until a violent gust blew it off its hook and it landed on the ground with a rude clang. The wind howled throughout the afternoon and evening, whistling under the doors, rattling the windows, and making Charlotte howl too. "I should comfort her," I thought. But I didn't. I couldn't move.

The heating had been on almost continuously, so the temperature must've dropped pretty low. All of a sudden, there was a particularly powerful wind gust and the heating went off. In my delirium, I waited for it to come back on but it didn't. I drifted in and out of a painful sleep, slowly becoming aware that the room was getting colder and colder. Finally, I hauled myself out of bed and staggered to the hall cupboard that contained the heating unit. I sank to my hands and knees, partly to check out the situation and partly because my legs wouldn't support me.

The wind had blown out the pilot light.

I knew I had to try to re-light it. Problem was, I'd never done anything like this before. It was unlikely that I'd have succeeded, even if I'd been in a fit state, which of course I wasn't. I tweaked about ineffectually with tapers and matches. There was a little voice in the back of my stuffy head, suggesting that a simple error on my part might blow up the house, but nevertheless, I persisted. A bunch of pathetic, worthless attempts later, I gave up. I honestly didn't have the energy. Frankly, I could've slumped to the floor right there and then, and slept exactly where I was except that it was already so cold my body was overcome with shivers, and the shivering frightened me. Picturing myself the star of a morbid Holiday headline, "Lonely Englishwoman half-eaten by household pets found frozen to death on hall floor," I dragged myself to my feet.

I took the duvet from my housemate's bed, hauled it on to my own, and crawled underneath. That was it. There I stayed. And that was where nature took over. When the room got so cold that ice could've formed on the windows, one chilly dog—and by "chilly dog," I don't mean "chili dog," I mean chilly *dog*—climbed under the covers and nestled up against me. I could feel her heartbeat; her gentle breathing and occasional snore were strangely comforting. When she warmed up, it was like having a hot, scratchy, slightly smelly brick alongside me. In my delirium, I hallucinated that she was the giant air-pumped snowman, and I came to with a start, greatly relieved to find her snoring and snuggled against me. One by one, the cats climbed aboard and settled in, a couple of them under the covers and a couple on top. During the course of the next few days, they swapped places. But all of them stayed with me and kept me warm. I felt like Nanook of the North, surrounded and protected from the wild by wolves and bears except that, in my case, it was cats and dogs . . . well, dog. I'm aware that they were keeping themselves warm, too, but that's nature at its best, isn't it? Balance. A win-win situation.

This was the scene that met Beth on her return after Christmas. My limp body under the bedclothes with her animals sprawled on top. She says she knew I'd fed them because there were open tins and dirty dishes all over the place, and, unless they'd fed themselves, it had to have been me. I had no memory of it, none at all. Did I get up to pee? Did the phone ring? No idea.

She asked why I hadn't called her. I dimly recalled trying, but the phoneline was out of order . . . maybe? Honestly, I thought I'd dreamed that. She said Katy had visited on Boxing Day to check up on me but when there was no answer assumed I was better and had gone out.

I used to believe that there was no particular happy ending to this story except that I was alive. Later I recollected that my English family's Christmas presents all arrived the day I got out of bed for the first time, and how overjoyed I was that they'd remembered me . . . you know how it is when you've been ill . . . emotional about everything! Also, Katy had left a box of gifts on the front porch that she and her family had planned to give me, so I had a cheery "festival of plenty" to open when I finally felt better. I celebrated my own private Christmas on New Year's Eve with Beth, a glass of eggnog, and those rock stars, Charlotte and the Cats. And, yes, Katy's gift was wrapped in purple-and-blue plaid.

Charlotte and the Cats

Chapter 16

Dad's Departure

In 1996, an event took place in Winchester in which I was not involved. I didn't know about it before it happened and only heard about it afterwards. I'm not sure who arranged it, and I only remember it now because there is a photo. If I'd been living in the UK, I imagine I'd have been included in the party.

On Boxing Day that year, my estranged father came to the family home for a Christmas visit. I'm guessing that Bro asked Mum if he could invite him so that Bro's sons could spend time with their grandfather. Either way, this time, he did turn up. I have a hazy recollection of Sis saying she'd felt ill at ease in his presence, and that the whole visit was uncomfortable. The word she used several times was "awkward."

A long Christmas Eve letter I wrote to my mother makes no mention of that event, and I'm certain I'd have discussed it with her if I had been aware it was on the schedule, because Dad hadn't stepped foot in the house since 1977. I've been unable to get more detail on the subject, as that part of our family history has been buried. None of my questioning has unlocked any doors, and my letters and diaries are not forthcoming.

In case you're wondering if I'm meandering aimlessly here, this event is noteworthy, other than that it happened around Christmas. I'd been tremendously disappointed when I discovered that Dad had been to our house, both because I'd like to have seen him, and because I felt excluded. I hadn't laid eyes on him since Sis and I had driven to his hometown to take him out for lunch some six years earlier. Even if he wasn't a huge physical presence in my daily life, I still loved and cared about him. Whatever he may have done in the past, he was my father and I missed him—at least, I missed what he represented—and I was genuinely willing to get acquainted, to "start again."

Thus, it was a wonderful surprise when he telephoned me in Austin less than week later, on New Year's Eve. It was about 6:00 p.m. (around midnight for Dad in England) when I was getting ready to go out myself. I tended to be rather nervous whenever I spoke to Dad, whether on the phone or face to face. I needn't have worried; it was a delightful conversation. We were terribly cordial and kept on safe subjects, never addressing our feelings or the past. He might've wanted to ask important questions, but he didn't like to pry. I longed for him to be interested in me and my life, but I didn't want him to pry. Too much water had passed under the bridge by then, too many issues had not been dealt with, and too many secrets had been concealed. So we kept it polite and, in retrospect, distant. But he did say how much he'd missed me on Boxing Day, and that he hoped we'd spend time together the next time I was back. My heart soared.

As I write this now, in 2020, I'm recalling an occasion many years before that New Year conversation, when I'd visited Dad in Salisbury, a city between Winchester and Chard. We'd both caught trains and met at Salisbury station before making our way to a pub for lunch. That day, I'd decided to take a gamble and ask him an important question; I wanted him to explain why he'd left us—the family, I mean. I was incredibly tense. It was the first time I'd ever met him on my own, as an adult. I was chirpy and witty and all-around likeable, the way I'd always behaved as a child, the way children tend to behave when they want a parent to love them, i.e., when they want a parent not to leave them.

I was determined to ask him my question. There was never going to be a better opportunity than this. When my chardonnay had loosened me up a bit, I judged the time was right, though I couldn't stop my hands from shaking, and my smile was rather forced. Yes, I was smiling. Let's keep things pleasant. Just as I opened my mouth to speak, he said, "Why did you get married so young? And to a non-Catholic?"

I was dumbfounded. This wasn't the way I planned it. He was questioning me? I swallowed and tried to catch my breath. And, before I had time to think, I said, "Because I loved him. And I was looking for a new family with a man in it. A father figure."

I couldn't believe I'd said that out loud. There was a pause.

"But I'm your father," he said, quietly. The whole thing was surreal, otherworldly. I couldn't breathe. I was outside my body.

"You were never there," I said.

Silence.

He stood up and went to the bar to get us another drink. I stared at his broad back, which was somehow so familiar to me, in a tweedy jacket, similar to jackets he'd worn when we were small. Dad was 5 feet 10 inches tall and was considered very handsome—to me, he had always been a gorgeous giant. Now he seemed slighter and lonely and vulnerable. My heart was breaking. I wanted to cry. I didn't want to hurt his feelings, but I had to ask him my question before it escaped forever. As he put my glass on the table, he knocked it, and a little wine spilled.

"Sorry about that," he said.

"Oh, it doesn't matter. It's just a little—"

"No," he stopped me. "I'm sorry about not being there."

I stared at my wine, spilled on the table. I was unable to speak. Unable to ask my question. That rictus smile was glued to my face, and I was struck absolutely dumb. And the next thing I knew, he'd changed the subject and my chance had slipped away. A barmaid came by with a damp cloth and wiped up the spilled wine, and that was that.

We walked each other to the train station, chatting lightly about nothing, and we never spoke seriously about anything ever again.

But sitting in my Austin apartment on New Year's Eve in 1996, though I was a tad nervous at the unexpected call, we chatted quite comfortably. As he signed off, he wished me "Happy New Year!" Then, out of the blue, he said, "I love you!" and I said, "I love you!" in return. We had never exchanged the words before—at least, not aloud—so it was significant.

Later, I was especially happy that we'd spoken those precious words to each other then. They became a great comfort to me when Mum called five days later to tell me that Dad had died suddenly of an aneurysm. He was seventy-one.

I flew back to the UK. We held a memorial service for this man we never really knew at what had been the Nason family church in Gosport, the town of his birth, then buried him with his mother and sister.

When my siblings and I cleared his tiny cottage—laughing and crying throughout the day, as is our habit—we found under his bed a suitcase filled with all the gifts we'd given him, and every single letter and card we'd ever written him, going back to our earliest childhood. That's a story for another day.

I never did get an answer to my question.

Dad, looking cool in one of his tweedy jackets

Chapter 17

Stone Broke Beef

"Such a bustle ensued that you might have thought a goose the rarest of all birds...Mrs. Cratchit made the gravy hissing hot; Master Peter mashed the potatoes with incredible vigour; Miss Belinda sweetened up the apple-sauce; Martha dusted the hot plates; Bob took Tiny Tim beside him in a tiny corner at the table; the two young Cratchits set chairs for everybody, not forgetting themselves, and mounting guard upon their posts, crammed spoons into their mouths, lest they should shriek for goose before their turn came to be helped. At last the dishes were set on, and grace was said. It was succeeded by a breathless pause, as Mrs. Cratchit, looking slowly all along the carving-knife, prepared to plunge it in the breast; but when she did, and when the long expected gush of stuffing issued forth, one murmur of delight arose all round the board, and even Tiny Tim, excited by the two young Cratchits, beat on the table with the handle of his knife, and feebly cried Hurrah!"

Christmas can be expensive. It doesn't have to be, needless to say, but if you're going with the "modern traditional" model—decorating house and garden, sending cards, buying presents, preparing enormous celebratory meals—it can cost a fortune. That doesn't include extras like buying cinema or theatre tickets, hosting parties, traveling elsewhere for the season, or meeting the dreaded store-bought Santa. How do regular folks afford it? Why are they content to be in debt because of it? I reflect on my early Christmases that tended to be modest affairs, centred around school and church, and whatever miracles Mum conjured up, and later Christmases spent with OPFs or groups of friends who became family by proxy. Such simplicity. When did the extravagance begin?

By the time I got to Texas, I'd begun to relish the idea of a "traditional" Christmas, though I wasn't so sure about the "modern" part. You may wonder what in the name of the Blessed Baby I mean by that. Do I know, myself? I'll try to explain. Over the years, I'd tried numerous options to find that elusive joy, only a few of which had succeeded, so I was inclined to fall back on old-fashioned ways: carol singing; long nature walks; holly, mistletoe and ivy; charades by the fire; small, thoughtful gifts; family dinners . . . you know, that time-honored dream.

But it was tough to retrieve the old ways, partly because I'd run out of ideas, and partly because none of my Texan friends seemed interested. Christmas was all about spending money—spend, spend, spend!—when I hardly had a penny to my name. Then a giant spanner was thrown into the workings of my little life, setting me off on another trail altogether.

In 1994, when I was thirty-seven, I married John, the same man I'm with to this day, though—as I've said—we're no longer married, making him rather dramatically my ex-husband-current-boyfriend, which sounds wacky for ancient folk in their 60s but there you are; we're baby boomers and we do what we like. Anyway, there doesn't seem to be a better term . . . partner, housemate, manfriend, lover, paramour, bit of stuff, main squeeze, old geezer, gentleman caller. What does it matter?

With our marriage, I was given the unexpected leading role of Wicked Stepmother to two adorable boys, one of my earliest character parts, at which I evidently excelled. I use the term "adorable" loosely because, though I was quite prepared to adore them, the same did not apply in reverse. I'm happy to state that we have a stable relationship these days. However, back then, my new charges, Beckwith (seven) and Eli (four) loathed me pretty much on sight. From the very start, family life was challenging and may be responsible for much of my craziness, and surely a lot of my therapy.

My new domestic arrangements didn't jive with my impression of how life might be with my own family, whether home-grown or ready-made. I'd pictured all sorts of wonderful scenarios, from enjoying their unstinting love, which I would of course reciprocate in spades, to giving them a little sister, the most precious gift I could possibly provide. But no such luck. John was divorced when we met; I was the first woman the children had had to get used to. Not only did they find this difficult, but also John was careful to ensure his own position as Loving Parent No. 1, so I didn't always receive the support I needed to become established in their young lives. And Christmas, well, what can I say? For my stepsons, that was still a special time they wanted to enjoy with their *real* parents . . . together, at the same time. Thus, John spent Christmas morning with them at their mother's house, while I investigated other activities for myself.

The hardest part of this was trying not to feel sorry for myself. I was increasingly aware of a familiar sense of desperation I'd sometimes felt in my childhood home and which had followed me through the years. As a result, I came to a momentous conclusion. I could either keep trying to force Mum's customs to work, then whine when they failed. Or I could combine them with a new set of traditions created especially for me, by me, and shut the f*** up.

On that first Christmas morning as part of my new family, after John had left for his ex-wife's house, I dressed appropriately and made my way to one of the Catholic churches in hopes of being uplifted by a Christmas Day service. This much would be similar to family traditions of my childhood.

Ah, Christmas Church in Austin, Texas. It was disappointing to find that, while there were services on Christmas Day, the kind of service I desired actually happened on Christmas Eve. In celebrating the day before, people could take the day off to be with family, rather than spend quality time with the Christ child and his family. What?! Didn't that defeat the object? I longed for carols and splendor and the inspiration one should find on the day itself, but apparently all that happened at various Christmas Eve services, from the afternoon children's service to the midnight Mass, which, as you may recall, was my chosen Mass in England, straight from the pub. That first year, I attended the St. Austin's Church* on the University of Texas drag. Regardless of how church was done in the US, I settled on my new Austin tradition: early service on Christmas morning.

After Mass, I'd put on my walking shoes, drive down to Town Lake (now called Lady Bird Lake) and hike the whole three-mile route. In those days, before Austin became the screaming, swarming chockablock metropolis it has turned into, it was still wonderfully weird* and walking around the lake on Christmas Day was a glorious spiritual experience in itself. A Christmas morning walk didn't seem to be a commonplace affair back then, and I was one of relatively few people on the trail. There weren't many cyclists out and about, crying "left" as they zoomed by, unlike now when it's like the flippin' Tour de France, even on a quiet day. There used to be lots of hippy dippies and oddballs and the like; frankly, it was hard to tell who was homeless and who was just odd. It's one of the things I've always loved about Austin. The strangest-looking people could be artists or astrophysicists or media moguls. Or they could be itinerant. On top of that, there was something so soothing and almost serene about the lake, I could almost imagine myself walking on a Sunday through the tranquil Water Meadows in Winchester or around the Serpentine in London's Hyde Park. Town Lake was so calming and mesmerizing, my imagination soared. I wouldn't have been at all surprised if Excaliber had suddenly emerged from the centre of it.

Even if the December weather wasn't as cold as one might like, the trees were still bare and there was a different light that seems to happen only on Christmas Day. I'm not religious as such, but if I call it the Christ-light, you may understand what I mean.

That first year, someone had lightly decorated a bare-branch tree with about a dozen silver and gold colored balls. I thought it splendid. It made me smile, and tears welled. The simple gesture was inexplicably touching. Alas, it has now become an Austin "thing." Across local hillsides and around the trails, families gather with carloads of tacky decorations, mostly home-made ones using paper plates, so that tree-filled slopes are a mass of fake, tasteless, artificial crap which looks ghastly and even uglier when it rains or it's windy. And just because they're often made by children doesn't justify it, sorry. To make it worse, no one bothers to clean up after Christmas so those poor natural wonders are left to look vulgar for months, even years, afterwards. I hate it. Get off my lawn.

After walking, I'd drive home and settle down with a nice cup of tea—the best way to comfort me when I need comfort—and toast and marmalade, and while *Chitty Chitty Bang Bang* played on the VCR (God knows where that tradition started—in my DNA perhaps), I would open presents received from my UK family and overseas pals. I'd unwrap as slowly as I could to make it last as long as possible.

Up to that point, my new customs went pretty well, but then I'd start to cry. I'd cry and pretend I was crying at Dick Van Dyke's trying to soothe his children at the loss of their beloved car, when it was really because I was lonely and very sad to be alone when I had a husband, who purported to love me, and new children, who seemed to hate me. *Stiff upper lip*, I'd say to myself, *stop griping*. Then my whiny voice would step in. *For the first time in forever, I have someone in my life and we're not together on Christmas Day.* And the sobbing would start all over again. Wahhhh!

John would spend Christmas afternoon with me, often sad himself because he couldn't be with his children all day, as he had been sad all Christmas Eve because he wanted to be with them then as well. And somewhere in all this, he'd get upset because he knew his sadness was also ruining my day. What a woeful twosome we were.

After the second year of this carnival of misery, which I acknowledge, in retrospect, as a balance of grief, disappointment, homesickness . . . and self-pity, that old chestnut . . . I was prepared to do whatever it took to be *busy* in December. So it was that in 1995, I appeared in my first all-singing, all-dancing production of *A Christmas Carol* for Live Oak Theatre (now Austin Playhouse) at the State Theatre on Congress Avenue, as Mrs. Fezziwig,

Laundress, and various party guests and carol singers. Austinites may remember the show, not because of me, but because the great singer-songwriter, Steve Fromholz, played Ebenezer Scrooge. To this day, I'm surprised and grateful that I managed to get cast because that show changed my life. Unbeknownst to me, it was the start of something.

As each of those early married years went by, John and I strove (I'm not saying "strived," so don't ask) to improve the Holidays. We combined ideas from our different upbringings and different cultures in an effort to create seasonal bliss. We did not triumph. I continued to develop new rituals to get me through tough times, especially when John and his ex-wife enjoyed the kids together, and I was alone.

Finally, one year, I had a brainwave. I was wandering through a local Austin grocery store—the very chic, very swanky Central Market—and noticed that they prepared an annual "celebration menu" with appetizer, entrée, dessert, the works. A lightbulb went off! Why shouldn't we, instead of a standard turkey dinner, prepare Beef Wellington with all the associated trappings? Something completely different! The flyer I picked up from the foyer provided every detail, from preparing duxelles, whatever the hell that was, to opening wine. For once, unbeliev-ably, the boys became animated by something we were planning as a family. The menu, as priced out by Central Market, was not cheap, but so elated were we to have inspired enthusiasm, we threw ourselves into the project with gusto, or to put it more accurately, we fell for it—hook, line, and sinker.

This is when I should share that John's business had recently failed and, while he wasn't actually bankrupt, he was flat broke, stressed by, and grappling with even basic bills. I was a "struggling artist" in the process of building a show-biz career with only a part-time job to keep the wolves from the door. I'd been planning to drop the part-time job and go full-time as a storyteller/actress. I wasn't yet destitute, but I was well on my way.

Instead of using H.E.B., our local supermarket chain, and choosing substitute ingredients, we made the rash decision to purchase everything from Central Market, exactly as described, e.g., designer beef filet steaks, smoked salmon, truffle mousse pâté, La Posada Spanish Sherry, Clawson Stilton, Boschetto al Tartuffo, etc. I still have the list. I break out in hives just looking at it. We bought it all, the whole shebang. We watched the running total at the checkout, eyes widening, jaws dropping, and we paid by credit card, because, let's be honest, there was no other way. We'll pay later, we thought, and we did.

Outside the store, sacks in hand, we were walking towards the car when John suddenly slumped against the stone exterior wall, and burst into loud sobs. I thought he was messing around, joking about the ridiculous situation we'd put ourselves in. But no. It was no joke. He placed the bags on the ground and put his face in his hands, and wept. I tried to comfort him, but I'm useless when others cry because I always start crying in sympathy. Finally, he managed to tell me that it was the meat, the price of the meat, the crazy stupidly high price of the meat, that had wiped the smile off his face. That's when it hit him. Our reckless fiscal behavior at a time when we were both nearly penniless. Now I was bawling, too. My desire for my stepsons to love me had led me to endorse something I knew to be foolish.

We couldn't have known, as we stood wailing outside Central Market, that the Christmas dinner that year would turn out to be the best, most successful menu we'd ever cooked, becoming the event of the season for the entire household, particularly the kids. They were incredibly excited, even eager, to help out: opening packets, washing vegetables, and chopping, glazing (and burning) pecans. The final results were not only delicious, but looked fantastic, too, better than the flyer picture. I can't reliably say why this was such a turning point for the boys, whether they felt relief that we were rich enough to afford such a sumptuous repast—we didn't tell them until much later that the opposite was actually the case— or whether they could see how hard we were laboring on their behalf. When I think about it now, their enthusiastic participation seems almost miraculous.

Those boys, currently in their thirties, do love me now and talk of that fabulous meal to this day. In fact, a few years ago, we prepared it again, this time for Thanksgiving, and we told the Christmas story at the table, laughing in a way that would've been impossible twenty years ago.

See Appendices

CHAPTER 18

The Road to Hell

"And now two smaller Cratchits, boy and girl, came tearing in, screaming that outside the baker's they had smelt the goose, and known it for their own; and basking in luxurious thoughts of sage-and-onion, these young Cratchits danced about the table, and exalted Master Peter Cratchit to the skies, while he (not proud, although his collars nearly choked him) blew the fire, until the slow potatoes bubbling up, knocked loudly at the saucepan-lid to be let out and peeled."

Donating money to a charity during the Holidays (no one in the UK calls it "the Holidays," but I favor the American gesture of inclusion) has become an annual event, a part of the status quo. And in Texas, where the state doesn't always do enough to support its poor and needy, Christmas charities abound. If you want to give, there are opportunities galore, helping to ease the guilt of the monied classes in their acute annual awareness that working classes will most likely remain right where they are—poor and needy. We Catholics, rich, lapsed, or otherwise, know that guilt well.

In the mid-1990s, still suffering from my annual Christmas blues, I cast my mind back to Mum's spirit-lifting ideas. Despite vivid memories of our crummy childhood charity experience, I now recognized that donating time, talent, and cash to a philanthropic cause profited both giver and receiver. Mum and I often debated altruism and whether it really exists, and we generally concluded that, as long as you act sincerely to improve another person's life and not just to ease your guilty conscience, it doesn't matter if both parties benefit.

I decided to follow Mum's example and chose a local Austin charity that arranged presents for seniors who were alone or house-bound or poor, or all three. I selected a lady from their list, let's call her Mrs. Smith. According to the paperwork, Mrs. Smith was asking for a dressing gown. Since it was a gift I'd choose for my own mother, this seemed not only doable but pleasing—and there it is already, me pleasing myself as well as my beneficiary. Anyway, I was to contact her directly and then let Laura, my liaison, know when the deed was done.

It's an understatement to say that Mrs. Smith was not espe-cially nice; brusque and rude would be better descriptors. "She's lonely and broke, but also proud," I told myself. I'd hit rock bottom in my life; I understood that. "Kill with kindness," my mum would say, so that's what I set out to do. After the initial phone call, Mrs. Smith wanted to communicate via email, which surprised me: older folk didn't use the internet much back then and computers were an extravagance for those without funds. Still, it made life easier for me; I often worked from home at my own massive desktop. Mrs. Smith was finicky about her dressing gown—style, color, size, preferred name-brand, even where to buy it. She knew *precisely* what she wanted. My husband, John, said, "She doesn't seem very grateful!" which did cross my mind, but I kept quiet; I shouldn't *expect* gratitude . . . I was trying to be self-less, remember? Then, without asking, she added slippers to her wish list. Expensive slippers. I took a deep breath. I was willing, but called the organizers to ask if it was common for wish lists to grow. No, they said, but they were okay with it if I was. However, I should keep them informed if she asked for anything else. Thus, even though I didn't have much money myself in those days, I noted her *precise* slipper details, too.

I purchased Mrs. Smith's present—the exact items she'd requested—from Dillard's at Highland Mall (now Austin Community College) along with lovely wrapping paper to make the packaging as special as the gift. When she gave me her address for delivery, I observed it had one of the better Austin ZIP Codes, and when I passed through the area on my way home from a work commitment, I saw that she lived in an elegant house with a cultivated garden in a rather posh neighborhood. Alarm bells were ringing—loud clanging Big Bens—because it seemed possible this lady wasn't as impoverished as she'd implied. "Don't jump to conclusions," I thought. "She might rent a room in the house . . . might even be the maid." I mentioned this to John, who thinks everyone's a swindler. "She's pulling a fast one," he mumbled.

Mrs. Smith instructed me to deliver on Christmas Eve afternoon. Never having done a charitable transaction like this before, I was anxious not to come over all "lady of the manor" or patronizing—English accents can give that impression. Simple graciousness and affability were the order of the day. I'd just knock on the door, hand over the gift, say "Happy Christmas!" —I mean "*Merry* Christmas!"—then beat a hasty retreat.

Perhaps trying to compensate for misgivings about her integrity, I spent hours turning Mrs. Smith's parcel into a magnificent confection that she'd be thrilled to open. Now, y'all know I'm not blessed with crafty genes—all right, I'm crap—so I devoted more time on her than my own family. My stepsons know how craptastically uncrafty I am; they have low expectations. Mrs. Smith may have been disadvantaged, but I intuited she'd expect a high-quality offering.

The day before the drop, Mrs. Smith sent a curt email that she'd like delivery earlier than arranged: lunchtime on Christmas Eve. A second message arrived, instructing me to deliver in the morning. Since my own Christmas Eve was already busy, and I'd expended way more time on her than was reasonable, I became frustrated, and called her. Mrs. Smith was very displeased.

"This is vexing," she said, terse. "Maybe you'd better come by tonight."

"I've already got plans for this evening," I said.

"You could leave it on the doorstep."

"No, I'm not available tonight."

She sighed audibly. "Well, how early can you get here in the morning?"

My stomach started to roil; my heart throbbed in my ears. I hate confrontation. "I'm not sure." I said. "I've got a lot to do tomorrow, its being Christmas Eve, but it's also my first day off in ages, so I was planning a lie-in."

She tut-tutted. "I need to have it as early as possible so I can pack it in my luggage."

What?

"Your . . . your luggage?" I said. "Are you going somewhere?"

If eye-rolling could make a sound, I'd have heard it. "Of course I am," she snapped. "My son is picking me up at 10 o'clock to take me to Houston for the week. If you turn up any later than 8 o'clock, it'll be most inconvenient."

My face had gone red with exasperation, I could feel it glowing! If I'd been a cartoon, steam would've been spouting from my ears. "Let me check. I'll call you back," I said, through gritted teeth. I was that close to shouting "YOU MISERABLE OLD COW!"

I immediately contacted the charity hotline and spoke to Laura about "Ol' Slyboots," as my husband now called her. Laura, trying not to laugh, instructed me to hold delivery. Later, she called back. Mrs. Smith had apparently "got the wrong end of the stick," believing the charity was a gift-bearing service for all and any old ladies that might want a Christmas freebie!

The hubster was nodding knowingly as I asked "Is there a nice old duck who might enjoy a dressing gown and slippers for Christmas?" But it was too late and everyone had already been taken care of, so I returned the items to Dillard's and gave a donation to the Sally Army.

After Ol' Slyboots, I steered clear of the elderly, and a few years later made my next attempt at supporting a cause, this time involving my whole family, i.e., my husband and his two boys—a "Blue Santa" operation, giving us the chance to adopt a family, make direct contact for a wish list, then deliver purchases personally.

I can't say that our kids were particularly enthusiastic about the idea. We planned to teach them that, while they themselves led entitled lives in a world of plenty, others subsisted with a lot less. They attended a private school for the rich and famous, to which they'd earned scholarships. On one hand, the school provided them opportunities for community service; on the other, it led them to believe we were disadvantaged. Their friends' families were so wealthy, we were deprived by comparison. Our younger boy once felt so hard-done-by, he stated disconsolately, "I'm the only person in third grade who hasn't been to Europe!" However hard the school strived to promote philanthropy, everything our kids learned apparently flew out of our middle-class windows the minute they got home. We therefore hoped they'd absorb a bit about ongoing service and love of community.

I keep saying "we" but I really mean "I" because, in truth, John and I weren't getting along, and we, as a family, were undergoing tough times. John's failed business a year earlier had left us almost as poor as the children believed us to be, and sharing his kids with his ex-wife was taking a toll on our marriage, particularly as they pooh-poohed most of my attempts to garner stepmotherly approval. John didn't have much enthusiasm for the Blue Santa project either, but I was so gung ho, he felt he couldn't refuse. Anything for a peaceful life. Recently, he told me he'd secretly agreed with his offspring that my plan came over as misplaced noblesse oblige.

We sponsored a family requesting a full Texas-style Christmas dinner with all the trimminses, as I grew up calling them, and gifts for three children. They resided on the eastside of town, known at the time as the area where many of Austin's underprivileged folks lived. Having worked as a storyteller in eastside schools, I'd usually encountered what Texans call "good folk" and come to appreciate that people could end up "low income" no matter how hard they worked. I especially liked the idea of hand-delivering because our kids would get a chance to visit neighborhoods they'd never seen before and offer generosity of spirit towards peers in less fortunate situations. I know, I know . . . the road to hell. . .

Our noble intentions sounded horribly embarrassing and condescending, declared the kids. It wasn't that they looked down on anyone, more that they were afraid the family would find our gifts demeaning and feel belittled by our well-meaning efforts at kindness—that's how they themselves would feel, my stepsons said, in the same situation. I understood, and I'd thought the same thing myself, but I also imagined that people who were down on their luck might appreciate friendly support to get them through hard times, and I genuinely wanted to help.

Thus, we dragged their sorry butts around our local supermarket to buy the wish-list vittles, and as their father lectured them on food prices and cooking on a budget, they rolled their eyes (giving Ol' Slyboots a run for her money) and groaned as only teenagers can. Hoping to neutralize Papa's seriousness, I shared lighthearted anecdotes of defrosting birds before cooking and rattled on about differences between traditional English dinners and American. God knows, those children would've stuffed in earplugs if anyone had offered them, and deservedly so. They were more helpful when it came to picking toys for the children, and, while I don't recall what we bought, we were satisfied that our chosen family would be pleased with the selection.

We'd contacted the family in advance. Delivery was to be Christmas Eve afternoon. Everything was boxed up and ready to go. It was a dismal day in Austin—on-and-off rain, and windy—not what one expects in the American south and, to be honest, not at all Christmassy. Our own house was warm and cheery as we packed the Plymouth Voyager, and colored lights on our Douglas fir shone merrily through the window as we drove off to do our festive kindness. It was not so jolly in the van. The boys sat in the back, and to say they were aggrieved would be an understatement: "How long is this going to take?" and "When are we going to Mom's house?" What they wanted to say was "You're ruining Christmas Eve!" All the wicked stepmother could offer in return was "This is an adventure!" and "We're doing a good thing here!" Alas, in spite of my incessant chirpiness, I was somewhat trepidatious myself.

The area we were visiting was as grey and cheerless as the weather. John got in and out of the van a few times, searching for our destination. It was buried deep in rows of plain, unadorned houses he called "Austin projects." To me, they resembled army residences, interim homes for military families passing through. There were few trees or shrubs, and those that existed, with their naked winter branches, looked as uncomfortable in the neighborhood as we were. Hardly a soul was out walking. No Christmas trees in windows, no twinkling lights to remind us that this was the season of joy. It was hard to believe that anyone lived there; it was so quiet. How could it be Christmas Eve? This was a ghost town, a no-man's-land, less than ten miles from our house.

We clambered reluctantly out of the van, each of us carrying something to the front door; the children held the wrapped gifts, my husband and I carried cardboard boxes with the groceries. He knocked. The door opened. The front room was in darkness, lit only by natural light from the windows. At first, it appeared that there was no one in the room; there was no movement. Then as our eyes got used to the gloom, we saw that the room was filled with people, apparently several generations of an African American family. Sofas and chairs had been pushed back against the walls, as if clearing the way for a party or show of some kind. Each seat contained a person. We were expecting maybe seven—grandparents, parents, children— four adults and three youngsters. But there were ten or eleven souls altogether, some standing against the walls. Maybe these were aunts and uncles, too.

Everyone was silent in our shared uneasiness. There was no jollity, no excitement, barely a reaction that I recall. It was as if we were to provide not only food and presents, but also an atmosphere. We had none to offer. We were nervous, awkward, out of place. For myself, the real discomfort stemming from the sense that I was lording it over someone, albeit inadvertently, must surely have been written all over my face. Perhaps our boys had been correct all along.

Don't get me wrong. We were thanked formally and profuse-
ly, and the children expressed gratitude for their gifts. And I think
it was genuine appreciation even if it didn't sound that way. What
was I expecting? The Cratchits with their affability and excitement
about the plum pudding, hot from the kettle? I really don't know.
Looking back, I see that I may have been expecting to be provided
with joy myself; that, rather than giving from my heart with no
need for anything other than the *pleasure* of giving, I wanted . . .
needed . . . the event to be an exchange of some sort: we give
you food and gifts; you give us a display of happiness that shows
your recognition of what beneficent people we are. In hindsight,
I'm sickened and ashamed of what I belatedly acknowledge may
have been seen as sanctimonious superiority. I'm equally horrified
by the notion that I was teaching our kids a lesson in kindness.
Bloody hell . . . the arrogance! John's actual words when we discussed it recently? We were "asshole white people."

Does altruism really exist? I can't answer that. I mean, even
now, I enjoy the thrill that comes from making a donation; I
don't seem able to stop it. I do hope, however, that in putting this
Christmas tale on paper, I've revealed myself to myself in a clearer
light and taught *myself* a lesson in humility.

CHAPTER 19

Ashes to Ashes

"Bob left the room, and went upstairs into the room above, which was lighted cheerfully, and hung with Christmas. There was a chair set close beside the child, and there were signs of someone having been there, lately. Poor Bob sat down in it, and when he had thought a little and composed himself, he kissed the little face. He was reconciled to what had happened, and went down again quite happy."

I've read that it takes a minimum of a year to get through basic grief after losing a loved one, because that's how long it takes to experience each anniversary at least once. Friends have supported that statement, and I learned its truth the hard way.

On Easter Sunday in 2007, my beloved mother died suddenly, unexpectedly, of congestive heart failure. She was eighty-one. She was found the following morning, Monday, 9th April, which is when I got the call. I screamed and howled. I was bereft and inconsolable.

Ten years after the death of my father, we held my mum's memorial service at St. Paul's Episcopal Church in Winchester in early May, and scattered her ashes a week later in Crab Wood, her favorite walking spot. As we completed our loving task, the rains came and the earth took Mum back. Ashes to Ashes.

We cleared the family home, a totally different experience from the clearing of Dad's modest abode, except that we laughed and wept from start to finish. Bro allocated assignments—I took care of mum's wardrobe and her huge LP collection (lots of Led Zeppelin and the Beach Boys)—then a house clearance company did the rest. And although major renovation was required after fifty years of Nason wear and tear, the house went on the market as is. I returned to Austin in time for Mother's Day. "How come mothers get a special day? What about us kids?" we once joked. "Mothers should get more than one day a year," she retorted. "It's children's day every day!"

As the months dragged by, I buried myself so deeply in theatre and storytelling that, in spite of an economic recession, I had a rare profitable year. Offers on our house came and went, then on 28th September 2007, we exchanged contracts. I was almost as devastated by that sale as I had been by Mum's passing. If she was the linchpin of my world, then that house was the sanctuary in which she held everything together. It added insult to injury. On 30th September—Mum's birthday and my first without her—I went to the Unity Church of the Hills, sat in the back row, and wept quietly all through the service.

The rest of the year was a living nightmare. First, those monumental losses haunted my thoughts and skulked in my dreams; there seemed no end to the mourning. Second, John's youngest boy left for college, leaving an empty nest. Third, despite couples' therapy, my troubled marriage deteriorated rapidly. And to crown it all, my mother-in-law, Mrs. P, who had relocated from Shreveport, Louisiana, and settled in an Austin retirement community, became a significant and ongoing feature of our daily lives. You might think that Mrs. P would fill the gap left by my own precious mum, but sadly, that could never happen. For Mrs. P did not like me, had not liked me since we met in 1993, and nothing I said or did made any difference.

My mother often offered weird, unusable advice. Sometimes, though, she nailed it. One such gem: "Newlyweds should never institute a custom of rotating his family then her family for the Holidays. They'll never be able to break it." This guidance was all the more apt in the US, which celebrates Thanksgiving *and* Christmas. I should point out: John and I had never started the his/her setup. My family were in the UK, so it made no sense, unless we arranged it well in advance. Once Mrs. P moved to Austin, however, it was expected that she would be included in every event we planned: Thanksgiving, Christmas, Easter, Mother's Day—the very dates I was now struggling with. I hadn't totally thought it through when I unreservedly agreed that Austin would be the perfect place for her to resettle. I'd assumed her presence would give me a chance to get to know her and give her a chance to accept me. Also, with John having four loving brothers and sisters, I supposed that, while we would accept our part in the cycle, there would always be the option of another family member helping out. But, in 2007, Mrs. P announced she would no longer travel outside Austin. There was no discussion; her family must come to her.

But no one wanted to come to Austin that year. John's sibs weren't available; they wanted to hang with their own children and grandchildren. Perfectly logical, yet it didn't seem quite fair. We'd hosted several Holidays with Mrs. P as guest of honor, where her comfort was highest priority. That year, that particular year, I hoped I might not have to be Mrs. Responsible, and take care of a lady whose presence did nothing but remind me how desperately I missed my own dear mum.

After extended conversations, John's younger brother agreed to join us. Layton and his girlfriend, Terri, arrived Christmas Eve. We hadn't discussed gift giving, but on Christmas morning, they gave us lovely, thoughtful presents, and we gave them almost nothing.

Mrs. P was collected and delivered in time for Christmas dinner. She hugged me politely then hardly spoke to me again. I served her a glass of chardonnay, and made sure the conversation was warm, friendly, and continuous—even when I'm having a problematic time myself, I can carry off the role of hostess with the mostess. Busy, busy, busy works for me.

When we sat down to dinner, Mrs. P scrutinized the roast potatoes I'd placed on the table. "John," she called, "I do hope you've made rice. You know I'm a rice gal!" She leaned over to Terri. "I'm from Louisiana. We don't care for potatoes."

"The rice is coming, Mama, and there's plenty of gravy to go with it," John said. I raced out to ensure rice was on its way. When all was ready, we said grace and tucked in. Other than rice and gravy, Mrs. P barely ate, moving food around her plate as if she were playing checkers.

As soon as knives and forks were set down, she said, "I hope there's dessert!" Knowing her fondness for fruit pies, a store-bought blackberry and apple pie was warming, and vanilla ice cream was to hand. But I decided first to offer my own favorite seasonal dessert.

"Would you like to try some Christmas pudding?" I said. John leaned down to explain what Christmas pudding entailed. She wrinkled her face. "Not for me, thank you, but I'll take a slice of pie." So I saved my pudding for later, and we all ate pie. There were seven at the table. This was my family, and I've never felt so lonesome. My eyes stung with unshed tears. Had I been four years old, I'd have yelled, "I want my mummy! Waaahhh!" Alas, that's less winning at fifty.

In a regular year, I'd have emailed my mother before going to bed to share my day, then phoned her on Boxing Day so she could commiserate. But she wasn't there. Instead, when the house had emptied of Christmas guests, and I'd cleaned and set everything back to normal with no signs of Christmas to remind me, I wrote her a letter to tell the tale. And then I tore it up.

CHAPTER 20

Scrooge in the House

Until recently, seventh-grade students in Texas had to read Charles Dickens' *A Christmas Carol* as part of their English literature studies. I've heard over the years how they dislike the book, and how they'd rather watch *Mickey's Christmas Carol* or *Mr. Magoo's Christmas Special* or *The Muppet Christmas Carol* than read something longwinded, outdated, and English to boot. "It's a waste of time!" they whine. "So boring! No one talks like that now!"

At least *A Christmas Carol*, being a novella, is one of the shorter books. I later discovered that those seventh-graders didn't even read the full-length version of the story, only the abridged version. Huh! They should count themselves lucky they didn't get landed with *Bleak House, David Copperfield,* or *Little Dorrit.* Now, those'll send yer average schoolkid into a coma.

In 1852, Dickens gave a reading from *Carol* in Birmingham Town Hall to the Industrial and Literary Institute; it was a great success. The next year, he performed an abbreviated version of the story in public, performing each character himself without props or costume changes. Thereafter, he read the tale a hundred and seventy times, until his final performance on 15th March 1870, the year of his death.

If I mention again that I've read the book every December since I was a teenager, that it's become the closest thing I have to a personal tradition, that I find truth and meaning in its joyful message, that I've acted in productions of it almost annually since

1995, you'll run for the exits screaming "Enough with that friggin' story!" However, I'd be remiss if I didn't share the one specific production that changed my own perception of its power.

Photo Credit: Christopher Loveless for Austin Playhouse

Other more famous actors (Hi, Sir Patrick Stewart!) had done it, but ever since I learned that Dickens presented solo readings of his own story, I had wanted to do it too. I suppose I should've been satisfied with acting in lavish productions at the State Theatre and Dougherty Arts Center in Austin, and the Stafford Opera House in Columbus, and on haybales in the Flatonia museum. I mean, I'd been Mrs. Cratchit, Mrs. Fezziwig, Portly Gentleman, Christmas

Past, Charwoman, Laundress, and sundry carol singers, beggars, and snowball-throwing children. What more could I want? Well, I wanted to present *A Christmas Carol* in its purest form, as a simple cautionary tale told by a storyteller. I wanted to play Scrooge. I wanted to play EVERYONE!

In 2004, I developed a youth production with the renowned Austin company Pollyanna Theatre, which gave me the idea of creating a storyteller version of the piece to take into schools and share with the infamous aforementioned seventh grade. I did just that, with some success, for five years.

Then in 2009, the chance of a lifetime came my way—to construct a one-hour one-person production of *A Christmas Carol* to be directed by Lara Toner (now co-producing artistic director) at Austin Playhouse. It would have a three-week run in the Larry L. King Theatre, a tiny black-box stage right next to the main stage.

Buckling down to edit the complete unabridged book—the word "delusional" comes to mind—I quickly recognized it was too much, so I worked from both the abridged version and my functional school script. I cut and pasted until I had what looked to be the ideal content, with only a few added lines to carry me through transitions. It was only when I reviewed my multitude of previous scripts from past *Carol* productions that I realized I'd ended up with the same basic play*.

Once Lara (LT) and I had agreed on the final script, our stage manager, Rachel, joined us, and LT's brother, Mike, commenced construction on a fabulous set with stairs, platforms, nooks, and crannies, so that furniture could be kept to a minimum. We wanted the show to be about my performance of Dickens' words—no bells and whistles, as Mum would've said.

LT had never directed a solo storytelling piece before, but she was an accomplished stage director and I've always loved her enthusiastic "Let's do it!" approach. I'd worked with other directors on one-woman shows and welcomed fresh ideas to lift my game. For me, it was a match made in heaven. I try to be minimalist when in storyteller mode, even when I'm acting out different characters. I like standing or sitting still to connect with my live audience, with short sections where two, perhaps three, characters interact. LT's initial idea was to add as much movement as possible—different characters in difference positions, blocking me as Scrooge and the other thirty-two characters in my *Carol* script as if there were actually thirty-three actors on stage. It was fascinating and ambitious, if a tad exhausting. But I respected Lara's direction, and it was such a blast working with that remarkable imagination of hers.

Needless to say, this coming from me 'n' all, it was only a matter of time before things went awry. During the last week of rehearsal, I caught a horrible cold that got steadily worse as the days progressed. I told myself that a woman in her early fifties shouldn't be so easily wiped out by a few germs, but I was performing a children's program of seasonal stories in schools and libraries during the day, and I was also dealing with a broken marriage. John and I had parted ways and the consequent sadness and anxiety meant I hadn't had a good night's sleep in months. I was often weary when I reached the theatre.

Each night, I'd arrive to find that Mike's set had progressed, giving more "areas" for LT to suggest I use: "Let's get you . . . erm . . . under that platform as Marley's Ghost, then up on that platform as Christmas Past!" or "How about you stand by the stool as Bob Cratchit and sit on it as Mrs. Cratchit! Can you go up and down during the conversation? Excellent!" Everything made sense, but there was a lot of movement, which I didn't mind trying, but which was getting somewhat muddy. Along with the extra action was the learning of lines, and the fact that my cold was worsening daily. I already had a runny nose, throbbing head, sneezing fits, and general exhaustion, and I now developed a sore throat and an evil cough. I was barking like a lifelong chain-smoker and, at the end of each rehearsal, my voice was shot.

Approaching the midweek final dress rehearsal (to be followed by preview, then opening night), it seemed only sensible to take serious drugs and reduce my symptoms, even it if meant getting through just the rehearsal before collapsing. Any presenter will tell you: it's a fine line between (a) being undrugged with streaming nose, sore throat, cough, headache, and fatigue, but being able to maintain your wits, and (b) taking heavy-duty drugs to diminish cough, ease throat, and dry up nasal passages, salivary glands, and other mucus outlets, while causing dizziness, inducing unconsciousness and totally numbing all functioning braincells. Oh, lucky me. Completely spoilt for choice.

Frankly, I was panicking. The whole production rested in my hands. I'd never missed a performance of a show, except on account of my mother's funeral two years earlier. My stupid cold had turned into bronchitis and laryngitis, and the lack of sleep wasn't helping. I'd pretty much known my lines before we started rehearsing, yet I was so ill, I couldn't keep anything in my head. Lara was kind and sympathetic, but she was panicking too. She had trusted me and my ability to do this—now I was barely operational.

Don Toner (DT), big boss of the theatre and LT's father, sat in on dress rehearsal to give notes. That night of all nights, I was at my unhealthy worst. You've had a cold-gone-bad, haven't you? Then you can picture the scenario. I took powerful cold medicine and, during what we'll loosely term "my performance," I displayed the disastrous results. I actually nearly fell over twice. It wasn't pretty. My heart was breaking for Lara. Her notes to me after DT had gone (he left before I was out of costume) reflected the misery.

On preview night, I entered the King Theatre, suitably drugged, to find Mike in the last stages of painting the City of London on the back wall. This was also Mike's first "solo" show, and his work took my breath away. There was St. Paul's Cathedral. There was Big Ben. The only things missing were Bert, the chimney sweeps, and some odd English accents! I was thrilled beyond measure. This was absolutely what I'd imagined when LT asked me to do the show. London is such an integral part of *A Christmas Carol* that it was if another actor had joined the cast. What a boost! Incorporating music, lights, costume and LT's amended blocking, this rehearsal was better, and most of the lines came out where they were supposed to. I was still sick, but I was getting used to the medication and its effects, and learning to deal with them. Certain scenes could still be marked "clunky," but I knew which ones and what needed fine-tuning over the next twenty-four hours.

We opened Friday, 4th December 2009. Health-wise, I was a little better. I had no school presentations during the day, and used my time to sleep, run lines (in my head, so as to rest my voice), and sleep some more. I've always suffered from stage fright and the circumstances of this production ensured I'd be freaking out by curtain time. Austin Playhouse has always been brilliant at packing the house for opening nights, and LT had worked extra hard to ensure I had a capacity audience for mine. I *love* having a full house on opening, though it fills me with gut-wrenching fear at the same time. I couldn't eat anything beforehand and got increasingly nervous when I heard folks chattering as they took their seats. As usual, there was the question of whether I'd lose the contents of my stomach, and, if so, when I rushed to the bathroom, from which end.

While Rachel was doing last-minute tech stuff, Lara gave me the customary pre-curtain speech: "Take your time, enjoy yourself, and remember how different it'll be with an audience!" Despite having heard it all before, I was especially moved—this was "our show" and it hadn't been easy. We hugged and she left to take her seat.

Then it was time. Rachel gave me "Places!" and climbed up to the booth. I pulled on my coat, wrapped my red scarf about my neck, picked up Scrooge's top hat and headed for the doorway from where I could hear LT make her curtain speech ("Now switch off your cellphones—you won't need them where we're going—sit back, relax, and enjoy Bernadette Nason as, well, EVERYONE in Charles Dickens' *A Christmas Carol*"). I watched the lights go down, and heard the opening strains of our old-fashioned brass-band version of *God Rest Ye Merry Gentlemen*. I took a few deep breaths—as deep as my body would allow—and stepped onstage as the lights came up. With a smile at the audience (*Oh, God, is that a full house?*), I removed my hat, coat, and scarf, and hung them on the wall-hooks. As the music faded, I adjusted my waistcoat, took another breath, and began:

"Marley was dead, to begin with, there is no doubt whatever about that. The register of his burial was signed by the clergyman, the

clerk, the undertaker, and the chief mourner. Old Marley was as dead as a doornail."

A ripple of chuckles swept through the space as the audience recognized those famous words. My first laughs! I was up and running. . . .

And within the next few moments, it happened. The joy of storytelling. The magic of theatre. The enchantment of live performance. Call it what you will. Storytellers know it, actors know it, and I was both right then. Everything whooshed into focus. Suddenly, I was transported to London. I was myself in London. I was Ebenezer Scrooge in London. I became Bob Cratchit and the Portly Gentlemen. I became all the characters, one by one. As I shared their adventures, I witnessed the immediate *real-time* effect that we, my fictional friends and I, were having in that small theatre. Travel with us to the City of London, we said, and they did! Our audience joined us in that extraordinary zone, safely captive in, and captivated by, the world of story.

Throughout the hour, the range of emotion I beheld was astounding. Some people grinned from start to finish, some cried. A few burly Texans, with tears in their eyes from the get-go, finally wept towards the end, when Scrooge attends his nephew's Christmas party:

"It's I. Your uncle Scrooge. I have come to dinner. Will you let me in?"

Let him in! It is a mercy Fred didn't shake his arm off. He was made welcome at once, at home within five minutes. Nothing could be heartier. Wonderful party, wonderful friendship, wonderful happiness!

And when I reached the last words:

It was always said of Ebenezer Scrooge that he knew how to keep Christmas well, if any man alive possessed that knowledge. May that be truly said of us, and of all of us! And so, as Tiny Tim observed, "God Bless Us, Every One!"

. . . there was hardly a dry eye in the house!

I'm waxing lyrical because it was such a fantastic night for me. It certainly wasn't a perfect show. Lord, no. I flubbed lines and forgot blocking—and there was one dreadful moment, while standing on a high platform with Scrooge and Christmas Past, where wooziness occurred—a combo of adrenaline, illness, drugs, and fear of heights—and I almost lost my balance, which would've caused a long tumble to the floor. I wobbled for a bit before catching myself and carrying on. That pumped the adrenaline, I can tell you! I accepted the standing ovation and curtain calls as my due for surviving opening night, knowing that it could only get better thereafter. However, there's no doubt that I count that evening among my very happiest. I finally felt as if I had found Christmas.

See Appendices

CHAPTER 21

The Great Texas Baking Fiasco

"Mrs. Cratchit left the room alone…to take the pudding up, and bring it in… The pudding was out of the copper. A smell like a washing-day! That was the cloth. A smell like an eating-house, and a pastry cook's next door to each other, with a laundress's next door to that! That was the pudding. In half a minute Mrs. Cratchit entered: flushed, but smiling proudly: with the pudding, like a speckled cannon-ball, so hard and firm, blazing in half of half-a-quarter of ignited brandy, and bedight with Christmas holly stuck into the top. Oh, a wonderful pudding!"

December 2011 was a shabby month in my neck of the woods. Four years had passed and I was still grieving over my mother and our family home. John and I had officially divorced, and I wasn't over that either. To make matters worse, we'd been unable to sell our house, so we were stuck in it together. Bro and I had had a significant falling-out, the repercussions of which were traumatic and ongoing. On top of all that, I was disappointed by a failed attempt to re-locate to Washington DC. Oh, woe was me!

As December approached, I made a fateful decision: to throw myself into a self-financed production of my solo interpretation of *A Christmas Carol*, which had enjoyed two years of success at Austin Playhouse. My supporters had told me they longed to see the show again and convinced me to re-mount it, but then hardly a soul showed up. I played to dismally meagre audiences. I get it: December is crazy busy; it's impossible to do everything. Still, it hurt.

Adding insult to injury, the City Theatre Company, Austin, which I was renting, was hosting its own production to follow mine on the evening line-up: an irreverent piece called *The Eight: Reindeer Monologues** and its audience was full to bursting every night. I'd leave my presentation, feeling exhausted from the intense hour-long performance and dejected that only, say, eleven people were in the audience, to witness lines of people queuing up for the late-night show. Once, I stayed to watch it myself. I didn't enjoy it—too crass and vulgar even for me, though I may have loved it when I was younger—but I had to acknowledge, this was what people wanted. One night, one of the *Reindeer* actors saw my performance before his, and had the grace to say, "It's criminal yours isn't better attended, bearing in mind you're offering a genuine *Christmas* experience, and ours is making a mockery of it." I appreciated that a lot, despite its making no difference to the bottom line.

But then, the worst happened. As my savings were being swallowed up by *A Christmas Carol*, my handbag (a lovely Italian leather number) and its contents (including new BlackBerry telephone, wallet containing driving license, INS card, and a large sum of cash, representing the last of my month's money, which I'd taken out that very day to buy presents) were stolen from my theatre dressing room while I was on stage waxing Dickensian to a handful of devoted followers about, to quote Jacob Marley, "charity, mercy, forbearance, benevolence. . . ."

Y'all know I didn't *want* to be glum at Christmas. I didn't *want* to add more misery to my preexisting condition. But I did feel hard-done-by, in the extreme. "How could you?" I shook my fist at the heavens. "How *could* you?!"

In the past, I'd always done something to change my mood, to lift my spirits, right? What did I always do first? What was my go-to activity? Yes, you got it! I'd read *A Christmas Carol!* Well, that obviously wasn't going to work this time. It was all I could do not to throw my script and the accompanying book onto a ceremonial bonfire. Thus, after closing the show that sucked every last dime from my bank account, I wracked my brains for a way to cheer myself up. Out of the blue, I recalled the Making of the Nason Family Christmas Cake*.

As you may recall from Chapter 3, Mum made the family Christmas cake in a particular way, sitting my brother, sister, and me around the washing machine in the kitchen to help. My POV is slightly different (though it always pleases me to note that our retellings aren't dissimilar). We sat around the washing machine because the 1950s kitchen in our Victorian terrace-row house was so tiny that it didn't have a table. The term "no room to swing a cat" comes to mind, but with my stout, elderly kitty sitting beside me, I shan't say it aloud. Anyway, our mum would pull the old Hoover-matic twin-tub washing-machine into the centre of the room—and when I say "centre," I use the term loosely, since the centre of the room meant the area you could stand upright without actually touching the walls—and place a tablecloth on it and three little stools around it, and there we sat while she made the cake. She'd measure out all those delectable ingredients—currants, raisins, sultanas, hazelnuts, almonds, walnuts, dried fruit, glace cherries—and before they went into the big brown mixing bowl, we'd each get a little handful. As the mixture was coming together, she'd pass around the wooden spoon so we could partake of the cake, before it went into the oven. No worry about germs in those days. Germs were good for you then. They built up your immune system, particularly with siblings.

The Making of the Christmas Cake was high on Mum's list of memory-creation ideas. It was an endeavor we loved, at least when we were little. Just thinking about it cheered me up. In the depths of my adult gloom, I wondered if by actually baking the cake, I could restore my waning spirits and recreate that same Christmassy feeling. It was certainly worth a try.

My sister had inherited Mum's cookbook containing the familiar cake, but I found a few fine English recipes online and also an excellent one in my Marks & Spencer cookbook. I planned to combine them, taking the best from each. They all suggested I'd need one hour to prepare, four hours to bake. I'll repeat that. Preparation time: one hour. Cooking time: four hours.

The next day, I bought all the ingredients at our local super-market. There were certain items which didn't fit the European description so I had to take a chance, e.g. flour. Who knew that flour was different in different places? I didn't. There were other things that I couldn't find at all, such as currants, glace cherries, and allspice, so I had to make substitutions.

Mum always said that making a rich fruit cake could be hard on the arms. I had a touch of carpal tunnel syndrome so I went to Target and bought a hand mixer. Since my various recipes used metric and imperial weighing systems—none of this American "cup" business for me, thank you very much—I got swept up in the moment and bought a set of old-fashioned weighing scales like wot they done used in *Downton Abbey*. Eat your heart out, Mrs. Patmore.

When I got home, I was shocked to realize that I didn't have a 9-inch baking tin . . . didn't have a baking tin of any sort. Was it really that long since I'd baked anything? Apparently. Had I never made cupcakes for my stepsons? Apparently not. Hmm. Perhaps I really was a wicked stepmother. Determined, I returned to the store and bought a cake tin.

The following day, my schedule was such that I could start at 5:00 p.m. and by 10:00 p.m., I would be leaning against the kitchen counter, brandy in hand, admiring my spectacular cake, cooling on the wire rack. As it turns out, I didn't have a wire rack but you get my drift.

At 5:00 p.m. on the appointed day, the three recipes were printed. All the ingredients were on the countertop. The kitchen was ready, and so was I. The show was about to begin. I took a deep breath, and the curtain rose.

My main recipe suggested that I first weigh out every single ingredient into separate pots. Darn it, I hadn't even unwrapped the scales. It was like Christmas already! Well, not exactly. It took me fifteen minutes just to cut the scales out of their box. And then, to get them operational, one had to build them. They needed to be put together, to be *constructed*. There were screws and bolts and balancing bits. I needed a Phillips screwdriver. After a fifteen-minute search, I hadn't found one so I tried using an ordinary one. No such luck. I finally shoved the scales back in the box and grabbed my pitiful selection of cups from the cabinet. Nearly an hour had gone by. Grrr! I made the sensible (read, time-saving) decision that there was no point in weighing out *everything* beforehand, just the important stuff like sugar and flour.

Next on the list was The Insulation of the Baking Tin. What? Apparently, the slow cooking of the cake meant that the tin had to be thoroughly insulated so as to avoid burning. I needed (a) parchment and (b) brown paper. I opened the oven-gloves-and-tin-foil drawer and there, to my great surprise, was parchment. Who knew? Now . . . brown paper . . . where would that be? None in the wrapping-paper drawer or the stationery drawer. Ah, yes, I know. Down behind the fridge. Booze bags. I had to cut them up and re-configure them (after shaking out the dried cockroach legs)

to fit the cake tin, and obviously I couldn't use Scotch tape because it would melt or something, so I stapled the paper together. Now to wrap it around the cake tin. This wasn't as easy as it sounds. I could see what the picture wanted me to do but I couldn't make it happen. I couldn't get anything to stay in place. What could I use that wouldn't melt/dissolve/burn in the oven? I resorted to wooden clothes pegs and paper clips. Can you say Rube Goldberg? Finally, I needed something on which to place the cake tin in the oven when the batter was ready to be cooked (which at the rate I was going would be the turn of the next century). The recipe recommended cardboard. I found an old pizza box, which I washed. Yes, washed. Don't judge me. I didn't want my cake to smell of pepperoni. Another hour had passed.

At last I was ready to do some actual mixing. Hurray! About bloody time! First thing in the process: butter and soft brown sugar. I'd already taken the butter out of the fridge (thank you; I'm not completely stupid) so it was soft. Rather than open a new packet of soft brown sugar, I decided as a cost-saving measure to use up the supply in my pantry which had been there for some time. Unfortunately, this soft brown sugar was not soft. It was the opposite of soft. It was hard and lumpy, like a big brown rock.

I went to my computer to look this up. Surely there was a way to loosen lumpy soft brown sugar. There was! I wrote it down, but before heading back to the kitchen, I checked my email and went on Facebook to tell everyone about my cake-making adventure. I posted a photo I'd taken earlier of the ingredients looking all pretty on the counter. I had to tear myself away from the pretty picture to return to the catastrophic real-life scene. The online de-hardification process involved warm, damp cloths and the microwave. Slowly but surely, I partially de-lumpified this ancient sugar. Time was ticking by! I didn't want to waste my whole evening so, ploughing on, I added the brown sugar *pebbles* to the butter.

I tried to mix by hand but, as Mum had warned, in no time at all, both my arms were aching. Having to bang on the sugar stones with the wooden spoon didn't help, of course. Ah, but I had a mixer. Darn it, now I had to get the new red and shiny mixer of out of its box; that took several minutes. It took another fifteen to work out how to use it, but once I knew what I was doing, I stuck its two wire whisk thingies into the mix and switched on. Bad idea. It seized up immediately on the brown sugar rocks.

After sorting out the mixer, I thought the addition of eggs might help the situation but however slowly I added them, I couldn't stop the mix from curdling. The Marks & Sparks recipe was *extremely* particular about the "no-curdling" issue, and big-time curdling was taking place. I added flour but it didn't help. And there were still these half-inch to one-inch sugar lumps to deal with.

At the three-hour point, I went at the cake mix with my marble pestle and mortar. Americans call it a mortar and pestle but to Brits, it's a pestle and mortar. I vented my irritations on those lumps of sugar; I slammed them like a hurt lover. I nearly broke my old-fashioned china mixing bowl, but the slamming helped both the process and my mood. With the heat from the oven, switched on since 5:00 p.m., the kitchen was heating up (as was I), so the sugar had begun to dissolve on its own. At least the electric mixer was moving freely now.

This seemed a good time to do what all first-class bakers do before moving onto the final stages of preparing a cake. I mixed myself a cocktail. A helpful gin and tonic.

Now was the moment to add the remaining ingredients. Having chosen not to measure them out beforehand, this part got a bit confusing, and the gin wasn't as helpful as expected. Each of the different recipes from different books from different countries had different amounts in different weights and measurements, which I hadn't taken the time to convert into stupid friggin' cups. There were different ingredients, too, as I'd got a few replacements when I couldn't find the exact item. One packet of dried fruit contained mostly dried apples and prunes which I'd never seen in a Christmas cake before. I'm not sure the addition of prunes would be necessary with all the raisins and sultanas. This cake-baking would not only be memory-making but bowel-shaking too.

Eventually, I dolloped the cake mix into the cake tin, and shoved it into the oven at 9:00 p.m. It was only after I'd closed the oven door that I realized I'd forgotten the brandy. Bollocks! Who forgets the brandy?! There was only one sure way to deal to this, something that all English bakers know. You "feed" the cake with brandy after cooking, when the cake has cooled down. While you wait for the cake to cook and cool down, you feed yourself with gin. I never actually saw my mother do that, but I'm positive it's what she would've recommended.

While eating toast and sipping gin, I watched Alastair Sim's *A Christmas Carol* twice through. I definitely felt a kinship with Mrs. Cratchit, comparing her efforts with her magnificent plum pudding, and mine with my soon-to-be magnificent cake. Then I compared the movie with my own show, and found it wanting, though that may've been the gin talking. Five hours later, at 2:00 a.m., the cake was ready and it was beautiful . . . rich, dark, and fruity. I was clever enough to take a photo to prove it. I began the brandy routine right there and then . . . one for the cake, one for the cook, one for the cake, one for the cook. I told Facebook that it took three hours to prepare and five hours to cook. That is a lie. It took nine hours from start to finish.

Once it cooled down, I was done; I couldn't be bothered to put marzipan or icing on it, because the cake didn't need anything else. It really was rather magnificent, when all was done and dusted. By the time I sliced it up into small pieces, it was more alcoholic than any cocktail I've ever tasted. I lovingly wrapped up each piece and offered them to friends and colleagues as a token of my affection, sharing the baking story at the same time. And you know what? I did feel a familiar glow of pleasure at that gift-giving exercise, the same inspiration I'd experienced when I sang *Hark, the Herald Angels Sing* at the Mayor's Carol Concert, the same gleam of insight as when I walked up Elm Road and saw the sparkling tree in the window of our home, the same thrill as when I made folks laugh at the Dubai panto, yes, the same wonderful high I got every time I closed a performance of *A Christmas Carol* and said, "And as Tiny Tim observed, God bless us, every one!"

*See Appendices

CHAPTER 22

Happy Blitzmas!

"In an old abbey town, a long, long time ago there officiated as sexton and gravedigger in the churchyard one Gabriel Grubb. He was an ill-conditioned, cross-grained, surly fellow, who consorted with nobody but himself and an old wicker-bottle which fitted into his large, deep waistcoat pocket."

Occasionally, I would have an opportunity to be part of a December show that wasn't *A Christmas Carol*. In 2011, the same year as my Great British Baking Fiasco, to acknowledge my volunteer work with Austin's Hidden Room Theatre, Beth Burns, the artistic director, gave me the starring role in a one-night thank you event, entitled *December Mystery Show: The Christmas Blitz of London, December 1940*. It was an exciting role based on a real-life person, Francine Agazarian, a World War II spy working with the Special Operations Executive.

Francine is a fascinating character and well worth a little research, and although there's quite a lot of data available about her now, there wasn't much on the internet at the time. Beth and I talked about it plenty beforehand. We wanted to be sure I had a handle on Francine's personality, as I was to improvise much of it, based loosely on Beth's script and what we knew of authentic wartime life at Christmastime, particularly during the terrible German bombing of England in December 1940.

Francine's story is beguiling, and in my research, I read deeply of the Blitz, the horrific German bombing of England that took place in the early years of WWII, and of the celebrated stiff-upper-lippery of my plucky compatriots. My mother's home-town of Newcastle was a target of the firestorm, and I longed to sit with her and sip tea and ask about her life; she'd have been in her mid-teens during the Blitz. Did she experience it personally? Was she affected in any way? But Mum wasn't around, and this is one of the many, many times that I missed her profoundly.

My American theatre colleagues and I created a world for the evening, based on what we knew of English wartime life, specif-ically at Christmas, specifically as it pertained to the frightening winter of 1940. The party was all the more authentic as it was held at the Hidden Room's regular space, the York Rite Temple in downtown Austin, a fascinating building on the National Register of Historic Places. Built in 1926, it had the perfect atmosphere for an event of this kind. I was gorgeously costumed in vintage gown with realistic hair and make-up. I rarely like my appearance, but the ladies who put together my look pulled off a miracle.

I'm hosting, as Francine, a social gathering at my London home for a large group of my friends— in my mind, it's 8th December, 1940, one particularly awful night of that month—and as the party begins, warning sirens go off, and the air raid begins. . . .

"Then the bombs came. . . . " it says in my notes.

I'm afraid I'll be out of my depth, improvising on the short script I've been provided by Beth, who was a performer and teacher at the Groundlings, a sketch comedy and improv theatre out of Los Angeles and who is therefore a bit of a whiz-kid on the subject. To be honest, improv scares me. There's a loss-of-control element that doesn't match my buttoned-up English self, but I've told Beth I'll give it my best shot, so away we go—

"It's an air raid!" I say, as loudly as I dare, to the gathered guests, who've been asked to participate as fully as possible in the spirit of the evening. They are dressed in wartime costumes, as accurate as they could contrive. The drapes in the room are drawn together to simulate the London blackout.

I take a full, life-affirming breath and, releasing myself into the moment, I breathe life into Francine's personality.

"It's too late to get to the shelters!"

The revelers, many of whom are local actors, directors, playwrights, designers from the Austin theatre community, are in character. They look aghast at one another.

"It will be my pleasure to entertain you here with one of my favorite Christmas stories."

Then I take the stage, which, in the main room on the third floor of the York Rite Temple, is a raised, red-carpeted platform, decorated with a huge Christmas tree. I assemble my audience as intimately as is possible, and pick up my book. I explain a bit about the Charles Dickens' story that I'm going to tell, and then I share "The Christmas Goblins"*. It's my goal to amuse and distract folks during the black-out as incendiaries blast around us. I like to think that I, in my guise as Francine, am doing well, that I'm an excellent hostess!

Photo credit: WillHollisPhotography.com

When the all-clear is sounded, wonderful actors in appropriate costume step forward to take over the entertainment, and my guests are taught the East Coast Swing. That's when the party really takes off. Remember, the invited audience is also dressed for the era, and they contribute to the merriment as if it's the real thing. My fellow performers and I observe that the presentation is so affecting, many participants are in tears. We've somehow captured the environment so exactly that our guests are right there with us, in that distant moment.

The room had come alive with boogie-woogie-ing and jitter-bugging, and I was still tingling with adrenaline. Relieved I hadn't made a complete balls-up of my improv bit, my thoughts drifted to my mum. What would she have thought of this event? Did she ever swing-dance like that? Had she kept a positive attitude when the whole world was exploding around her? I desperately wanted to ask her. I so wished she were by my side. All of a sudden, as if from nowhere, something passed over me—a wave, a shadow, a breeze, perhaps from one of those fabulous dresses swinging on the dance floor—and every hair on my body stood on end. Ha! Maybe she was. . . .

See Appendices

CHAPTER 23

The Most Christmassy Town in the Whole Wide World

"The sight of these poor revellers appeared to interest the Spirit very much, for he stood with Scrooge beside him in a bakers doorway, and taking off the covers as their bearers passed, sprinkled incense on their dinners from his torch. And it was a very uncommon kind of torch, for once or twice when there were angry words between some dinner-carriers who had jostled with each other, he shed a few drops of water on them from it, and their good humour was restored directly. For they said, it was a shame to quarrel upon Christmas Day. And so it was! God love it, so it was!"

Out of the blue, my sister snail-mailed me an English newspaper, which declared that Winchester "has been battling York for the coveted title of 'Most Christmassy Town in Britain.'" Really? You coulda knocked me over with the proverbial. Winchester is a beautiful city, and my hometown memories are potent, but "the Most Christmassy Town in Britain"?

I suppose it was inevitable that I'd eventually wish to return to the place where it all began and give Christmas another shot from home base. For the first time in twenty-six years, I'd be "home for the Holidays." I was pushing thirty when I was last in the UK for 25th December, back in 1986, between Libya and Dubai. Now, at the seasoned age of fifty-five, nearly half a lifetime later, I was heading to ground zero to see for myself. Of course, strictly speaking, "home base" no longer existed, which meant I'd need to find other places to stop over.

My siblings had shown vague enthusiasm when I first mentioned my visit, welcoming the idea in the way of undemonstrative families the world over: kind, but distant, with a soupçon of "How long's she staying?" Sis had agreed I could spend half the time in her modest bungalow, despite her getting claustrophobic when anyone shared her space for longer than an hour. My brother, with whom I'd just reconciled after a two-year rift, agreed I could stay with him and his wife for the latter half of my trip.

After closing my December run of *A Christmas Carol* at Bastrop Opera House, I flew to Blighty. Sis met me at the airport, a tradition going back to my Libya days, and as always, I was champing at the bit to disembark, grab my luggage, and zip through Heathrow Customs so I could embrace her again. And there she was! At first sighting we waved like wackos, screaming each other's names across the airport, as in a movie, and jostling past bystanders to reach one another. The hugs were short (Nason-style) but the conversation, immediate:

"How was the flight?"

"Fine, apart from the crying baby and having to pay for my G&Ts. What time did you get to the airport?"

"About 4 o'clock."

"You're kidding! Four hours early? Why?"

"Oh, you know me. I couldn't sleep properly for worrying that the alarm wouldn't go off, and after 2 o'clock, I couldn't get back to sleep at all. Then I panicked that I'd forgotten the way to the airport, so I decided I might as well set off and have a coffee at Costas when I arrived. Of course, it only took an hour at that time of night so I've had three coffees, an orange juice, and a croissant. Actually, speaking of that. . ."

"You need to pee, right?"

"Right. Do you need to pee?"

"Why not? I'm sure I can find a little pee up there somewhere. . . ."

After using the loo and wincing at my bedraggled appearance in the unforgiving airport mirrors—my skin needed washing and ironing more than my clothes—I found Sis adjusting my bags on a trolley, and we zigzagged around fellow travelers towards the parking garages. She'd written down some parking details (level, row, etc.) so we wouldn't spend more time hunting down her car than I'd spent on the flight (as had happened in the past), but she couldn't recall which of the many garages she was in. It took an hour. By the time we retrieved the car and squeezed my bags inside it, I was tired and irritable, and so was she. Again, par for the course. This took place every time she met me at the airport, so I should have been used to it, but I wasn't. I'll never get used to it. Sis and I are alike in many ways (and almost like twins to look at, except she's fair with blue eyes and I'm dark with hazel eyes . . . well, I'm a redhead these days, and I imagine we're both grey now, but you know what I mean) but there are multiple fields in which we're diametrically opposite. Parking at airports is one of them.

And there, twenty-six years on, in my sister's car, passing through majestic south England countryside en route to Winchester, the morning sun rising behind us, I learned with a sinking heart that Nason Family Christmases had been modified. Like our mother before her, Sis liked to work on Christmas Day; she was a cook (*never* call her a chef!), and restaurant and pub kitchens were busy at Christmas because nowadays the public increasingly enjoyed eating out, way more than in the past, and definitely more than in our childhood. As I was staying with Sis for the Day part of Christmas, this meant I'd spend it alone. Hmph. Bro and wife, it transpired, were also never home on Christmas Day. They dined at a fancy restaurant, having added this custom to their celebratory schedule many years earlier. It was their tradition.

Thus, on a drizzly Christmas morning, after a subdued present opening which seemed to depress her, Sis left for her tour of duty, and I was alone. In general, I like being alone, but fully alone on Baby Jesus Day was unique, even in my troubled past. I've never been a huge fan of Gordon Ramsay, finding him unnecessarily rude for the sake of ratings, but I passed my morning watching him produce an elaborate Christmas lunch for his friends and family (wishing they were my family) and sincerely appreciating his brisk bonhomie.

The afternoon found me wandering the rainy deserted streets of downtown Winchester singing "Hark, the Herald Angels Sing" in the pouring rain. It was the wettest, dreariest winter in years (no snow, natch) and as I'd arrived too late to appreciate the city's seasonal events, there wasn't anything to see or do. I was sorely tempted to plant myself outside the cathedral and belt out a few carols, but could already imagine the headlines of next week's Hampshire Chronicle: *Multiple complaints lead to arrest of unhinged ex-Winchester woman for disrupting the peace on Christmas Day. The crazy carol-singing woman has been confined in Moorgreen Psychiatric Unit, pending mental health tests and deportation.* I did, however, derive some pleasure from the jolly twinkling trees in OPF's windows. "Deck the halls with boughs of holly, fa la la la la, la la la la!" I sang (quietly, to myself), wondering if anyone else was having as strange and melancholy a day as I.

Christmas tree in window of Cheyney Court, Winchester

On Boxing Day, as a special treat, I bought tickets for Sis and me to see the panto—that year it was *Aladdin*—at the Theatre Royal Winchester.

"Let's relive our childhood!" I said, excitedly.

"I don't think we went to the panto much, did we?"

"Mum took us several times. It was one of her things."

"Was it? I don't really remember that."

I let the subject drop, noting that our memories of Christmas pasts were poles apart. We settled in our front-row seats, and as soon as the curtain lifted, I was involved, participating at every opportunity, and yelling back like a big kid, as panto convention dictates: "Look behind you!" "He's *behind* you!" "Oh, no he isn't!" "Oh, yes he is!"

Sis sat as still as a mouse. I elbowed her.

"Come on, join in!"

She gave me a sickly smile. "But it's all so *silly*," she said. "It's for little kids!"

"Let your hair down," I said. "It's fun!"

But it wasn't fun for her, that was obvious. It simply wasn't her thing; I understand that now, and in other circumstances, I've felt the same way. She was bored stiff. After downing her intermission gin and tonic—it had only two half-melted lumps of ice, so downing it was easy—she slid a ten-pound note across the table, saying, "Here's your taxi fare home. I'm off!" And she bolted before I had a chance to shout, in true panto-style, "Oh, no you're not!"

Lest you find my sister's sudden departure cruel or insensitive, I should tell you that, while I was a bit disappointed she wasn't getting a kick out of the show, her reaction wasn't offensive. First, when you're close to someone, you want them to be happy. She thought I'd be happier on my own, that by pretending to enjoy something that bored her, she'd make me uncomfortable. For myself, I'd grown out of forcing her to do something she didn't like. Second, quick exits from places or events that we're not enjoying is in our family DNA. My siblings and I inherited the "I've got to get out of here or I'll have a panic attack!" response on both our dynastic lines. Our parents suffered with claustrophobia in equal measure; it became progressively more noticeable as they aged. Mum would say, "Life's too short to be doing something you really don't want to do," before making a run for it. At least Sis paid my cab fare!

I returned the following year, taking John—by this time, my ex-husband current boyfriend—as moral support. Wait. . . what?! Yep, you read right. After four years spent apart while still living in the same house, we had rekindled our romance, revitalized our relationship and started reestablishing familial ties. It took some intense therapy, but we did it. Thus, we took a chance on a vacation with my family, arriving on Christmas Eve when *all* festivities had concluded. The cheery local pubs became our solace when my sibling's jolly diversions continued: Sis left town to visit a friend on Christmas Day; Bro and wife dined out, as usual. My first reaction was to mourn the loss of the Holidays I'd hoped for, to long for childhood Christmases, as I did so often. Then, in a pub conversation, John reminded me of something.

"Those old Christmases weren't especially good, were they? I mean, they were often quite gloomy. At least, they've always sounded that way to me."

I couldn't disagree with that.

"You never knew if your dad was going to appear. You kids were anxious about your mum, and each other too. Y'all were probably disguising how you really felt, putting on a brave face."

"And Mum was always struggling," I said, "creating things to make our day better, sort of faking it in the hope of making it. . . ."

As the beer flowed, John and I hashed out those early Christmases to see if we could make sense of them. This was our conclusion: every December since childhood, I'd been recalling and then attempting to relive the memories that Mum had striven to install in our young minds. Because I was afraid of the alternative, that if I gave myself approval to consider that Mum's methods didn't actually work, I wouldn't know what to do. I'd never get over it.

"Mum was successful in her mission, then," I said, "because I'm always trying to do what I believe she'd have done, recreating something that may well have been disagreeable, a Happy Christmas that perhaps didn't exist. I've been subconsciously coercing my sibs and my friends and your kids to go along with it. And you. Because if I can make us do the same things, I can pretend we're having a merry time."

John nodded slowly at my general thought process. If he could've, he would've broken into song à la Henry Higgins—"By George, I think she's got it!"—and I would've swayed around the bar (some Winchester bar) singing, "I could've danced all night!" Okay, it wasn't as momentous as that, obviously. John's not the big musical fan I'm constantly pressing him to be. And, frankly, that specific conversation lasted for hours as we crawled from pub to pub, and we were a bit pissed, and we'd had the same conversation a billion times over the years, and there's been some therapy. But his slow nod meant a lot. I slow-nodded a bit myself.

As a result, I began a gradual personal shift, adjusting old habits, and taking steps to release others from the visions I'd had since childhood. Again, this wasn't immediate—I was as plodding as a tortoise crossing Salisbury Plain—but I was determined. I had new mantra: "I must not force my Concept of Christmas on others."

With John at one of the many pubs we visited

Third time's a charm. Three years later, an earth-shattering decision was made: WE SHALL STAY IN HOTELS! That choice alone partially solved my conundrum: no forced joviality, no claustrophobia, and, in keeping with modified schedules, only small doses of kinfolk. Instead, huge dollops of alternative people to see, things to do, and places to go.

That year, the weather forecast had suggested that snow was a possibility, raising hopes to high levels. There was no snow. Instead, we experienced rain, rain, and more rain. Worse, there were storms, with torrential downpours and wind gusts the likes of which I'd never experienced on the south coast before. I was forced to agree with tourists who say "Dadgummit, England, what's with all the rain?!" I finally understood.

John and I managed once again to miss most of the events that Winchester had to offer, though the German market* had a few days to run. The weather was so appalling, we didn't witness the market at its best. Shoppers were grim-faced, waging war with umbrellas, packages, and other punters, yet shopkeepers remained steadfastly chirpy, and there was a low-level air of excitement. One could sense how lovely it would be with blue skies and sunshine, or even better, snow.

Hotels are obviously way costlier than staying with relatives, but the Premier Inn Winchester* was a thrifty option that turned out so well, we invited Sis for Christmas breakfast and had a splendid—and distinctive—start to our Christmas Day. Sis went to work, and John and I ambled to the cathedral for a spot of spiritual succor, just like Mum. Then we walked in the rain to Sis's place to prepare the big meal. When she got back, we toiled in shifts in her teeny-weeny kitchen and ate our roast in front of the telly. It was pleasing, truly. Afterwards, we took a constitutional, the three of us, back into town, parting ways near the Buttercross, the central point of Winchester High Street. From there, John and I continued to our hotel and Sis marched home, brolly in hand, insisting that it was safe, as it turned out to be. I'd never had a Christmas quite like it.

Clearly having forgotten my good intentions, we dragged my sister on an adventure she'd agreed to have, but which on the day she didn't want—a trip to Highcliffe-on-Sea* with her as driver. A tempest was raging, the rain was bucketing down, but still John and I wanted to go. It was not a cheerful visit; another example of pressuring a family member to carry out one's wishes—big sister bullies baby sister here. The photos of our expedition imply that a carefree time was had by all when in fact Sis was sullen, start to finish. When we talk about it now, our reminiscences make us laugh, so it wasn't a complete wash-out (forgive the pun) and at least I didn't insist she do anything Christmassy, which is what I'm going on about here.

To my great delight, John volunteered to accompany me to that year's panto: *Cinderella*. He wore a suit and tie, and treated our evening with the respect it deserves. He assures me that he enjoyed the occasion from start to finish, pleased to view firsthand the spectacle I'd been yabbering on about for twenty-five years. Personally, I don't believe he loved the actual performance, though it's possible that the cocktails he consumed before and during the show may have loosened his high artistic aesthetic.

For me, this change in old patterns, this *shift*, altered everything. Although it wasn't always easy, I came to accept that my family had shaped their own lives during my quarter-century absence and that my efforts to impose on them the Christmas I claimed I wanted was as much of a strain on them as it was on me. I fear this will sound corny and that more mature folk will roll their eyes disparagingly, but I attained a kind of inner peace that I always considered beyond me. In my newly enlightened eyes, Winchester had indeed ended up being the most Christmassy town in the whole wide world, without doing a damn thing!

York won, by the way.

See Appendices

CHAPTER 24

The Perfect Christmas — A Solstice Smash

"I will honour Christmas in my heart and try to keep it all the year. I will live in the past, the present and the future. I will not shut out they lessons they teach."

A nd now, every year, I celebrate perfect Christmases that match my new understanding of exactly how festivities should go. Lord, don't be silly. Utter bollocks. Of course I don't. Have you been drinking? There's no such thing as a perfect Christmas. It's just a day, just one day out of the whole year. And that day, let's be honest, is a fusion of many dates and events on or around 25th December (only one of which—the Solstice—is based on fact) that somehow ended up in the beautifully-wrapped beribboned giftbox that we now call Christmas. Besides, if all my research is reliable, no one really knows for sure when Jesus Christ was born. There, I said it.

Let's remember that the celebration of Christmas, at least in Britain, was dying out when Charles Dickens brought it back into fashion with *A Christmas Carol* in 1843. The first commercial Christmas cards, as we've come to know them, also appeared in 1843 to support the Penny Post, which had been implemented three years earlier. Queen Victoria and Prince Albert decorated their first tree and introduced it to the British Empire in 1848. America has even more to answer for, giving us Santa Claus: a sleigh riding, gift-giving, chubby, white-bearded gentleman in a bright-red outfit trimmed with white fur. From a historic

4th-century Greek saint, known for secret gift-giving, through Clement Moore's "A Visit from St Nicholas" in 1822, through the artistic vision of Thomas Nast in 1867, to Norman Rockwell in the 1920s and 1930s, dear Santa has morphed into the gleeful snazzy-suited dude we recognize today.

As far back as I can recollect, I've been fostering an image of a perfect Christmas that came into being in the mid-1800s. But it doesn't exist in the real world—it's an illusion—and it has never existed in my own life, childhood or adulthood, however hard my beloved mother tried to create it. It's no one's fault. There's no blame. I just wanted that perfect Christmas because it meant love and family and friendship and warmth and comfort and kindness and generosity and all the other things I so desperately needed as a child, things that weren't always there. I accepted the illusion—and continued to chase it throughout my life—because I desired it so very much.

These days, I acknowledge that my mother's traditions are fine as a base, as a foundation for festivities, but can't be the whole thing, i.e., they work as tools but aren't Christmas in and of themselves. I've been trying to recreate the childhood Christmas I dreamed of, one that I somehow believed I had, but never actually did. Using old images stored in my memory as if they were the real thing, I've been struggling to build a reality that never actually existed.

Here's an idea: why not think of every day as Christmas Day? I mean, the reason people love Christmas is that it encourages kindness and generosity, and people want to experience kindness and generosity every day of the year, don't they? Not just for one month, building up to one day. That's why folks start so early, why they can't wait to get through the summer, why they're pumping up the garden reindeer before the Halloween ghosts have cleared the lawn. That's the reason there's a year-round Christmas Store, and Lala's Little Nugget* hosts St. Nick's birthday in March and Christmas in July. Let's celebrate every day as if it were Christmas. That's all I'm saying.

You'll vomit if I say, "Life is what you make it," but that's what I'm coming to believe; that's why the cliché exists. Well, Christmas is what you make it, too.

So I'm adapting. Wise old crone that I am, I'm acknowledging here and now that our modern celebration doesn't reflect the Charles Dickens' morality tale I've been trying to live up to, and that none of it—indeed, nothing in life—has anything to do with what I display on the outside, but everything to do with a feeling in my heart. There's no avoiding it, you see; I'm going sentimental on you, whether you like it or not. Now get over it and pass me the eggnog.

Happy Christmas, everyone! Merry Christmas, y'all!

Quotations lifted with thanks from
A Christmas Carol by Charles Dickens

"And it was always said of him, that he knew how to keep Christmas well, if any man alive possessed the knowledge. May that be truly said of us, and all of us! And so, as Tiny Tim observed, God Bless Us, Every One!"

*See Appendices

The Christmas Goblins

by Charles Dickens

I n an old abbey town, a long, long time ago there officiated as sexton and gravedigger in the churchyard one Gabriel Grubb. He was an ill-conditioned, cross-grained, surly fellow, who consorted with nobody but himself and an old wicker-bottle which fitted into his large, deep waistcoat pocket.

A little before twilight one Christmas Eve, Gabriel shouldered his spade, lighted his lantern, and betook himself toward the old churchyard, for he had a grave to finish by next morning, and feeling very low, he thought it might raise his spirits, perhaps, if he went on with his work at once.

He strode along 'til he turned into the dark lane which led to the churchyard - a nice, gloomy, mournful place into which the towns-people did not care to go except in broad daylight. Consequently he was not a little indignant to hear a young urchin roaring out some jolly song about a Merry Christmas.

We wish you a Merry Christmas;
We wish you a Merry Christmas;
We wish you a Merry Christmas and a Happy New Year.
Good tidings we bring to you and your kin;
Good tidings for Christmas and a Happy New Year.

Oh, bring us a figgy pudding;
Oh, bring us a figgy pudding;

Oh, bring us a figgy pudding and a cup of good cheer
We won't go until we get some;
We won't go until we get some;
We won't go until we get some, so bring some out here

Gabriel waited until the boy came up, then rapped him over the head with his lantern five or six times to teach him to modulate his voice.

"Modulate your voice, you little whippersnapper. In fact, don't sing at all. I don't like it!"

And as the boy hurried away, with his hand to his head, "Owwww!" Gabriel Grubb chuckled to himself,

"He he he!" and entered the churchyard, locking the gate behind him.

He took off his coat, put down his lantern, and getting into an unfinished grave, worked at it for an hour or so with right good will. But the earth was hardened with the frost, and it was no easy matter to break it up and shovel it out. At any other time this would have made Gabriel very miserable, but he was so pleased at having stopped the small boy's singing that he took little heed of the scanty progress he had made when he had finished work for the night, and looked down into the grave with grim satisfaction, murmuring as he gathered up his things:

"Brave lodgings for one, brave lodgings for one. A few feet of cold earth when life is done."

"He he he!"

And he carried on laughing, as he set himself down on a flat tombstone, which was a favorite resting-place of his, and drew forth his wicker-bottle.

"A coffin at Christmas! A Christmas box. He he he!"

"He he he!" repeated a voice close beside him.

Gabriel looked all about him but there was nothing to be seen.

"It was the echoes," he said, raising the bottle to his lips again.

"It was not," said a deep voice.

Gabriel leapt to his feet and stood rooted to the spot with terror, for his eyes rested on a form that made his blood run cold.

Seated on an upright tombstone close to him was a strange, unearthly figure. He was sitting perfectly still, grinning at Gabriel Grubb with such a grin as only a GOBLIN could call up.

"What do you here on Christmas Eve?" said the goblin, sternly.

"I, um, I came to dig a grave, sir," stammered Gabriel.

"Tut, tut, tut! What man wanders among graves on such a night as this?"

"Gabriel Grubb! Gabriel Grubb!" screamed a wild chorus of voices that seemed to fill the churchyard.

"What have you got in that bottle?" said the goblin.

"Hollands, sir," replied the sexton, trembling more than ever, for he had bought this Dutch gin from smugglers, and he thought his questioner might be in the tax-and-excise department of the goblins.

"Who drinks Hollands alone, and in a churchyard on such a night as this?"

"Gabriel Grubb! Gabriel Grubb!" exclaimed the wild voices again.

"And who, then, is our lawful prize?" exclaimed the goblin, raising his voice.

"Gabriel Grubb! Gabriel Grubb!" replied the invisible chorus.

"Well, Gabriel, what do you say to this?" said the goblin, as he grinned a broader grin than before.

The sexton gasped for breath and was unable to answer.

"What do you think of this, Gabriel?"

"It's--it's very curious, sir, very curious, sir, and very pretty," replied the sexton, half-dead with fright. "But I think I'll go back and finish my work, sir, if you please."

"Work!" said the goblin, "what work?"

"The grave, sir."

"Oh! the grave, eh? Who makes graves at a time when other men are merry, and takes a pleasure in it?"

"Gabriel Grubb! Gabriel Grubb!" replied the voices once more.

"I'm afraid my friends want you, Gabriel," said the goblin.

The sexton was horror-stricken. "Under favor, sir, I don't

think they can; they don't know me, sir; I don't think the gentle-men have ever seen me."

"Oh! yes, they have. We know the man who struck the boy in the envious malice of his heart because the boy could be merry and he could not."

Here the goblin gave a loud, shrill laugh which the echoes returned twenty-fold.

"I—I am afraid I must leave you, sir," said the sexton, making an effort to move.

"Leave us!" said the goblin laughing loud and long. And as he laughed he suddenly darted toward Gabriel, laid his hand upon his collar, and sank with him through the earth. And when Gabriel had had time to fetch his breath he found himself in what appeared to be a large cavern, surrounded on all sides by goblins ugly and grim.

"And now," said the king of the goblins, his new friend from the churchyard, now seated in the centre of the room on an elevated seat, "show the man of misery and gloom a few of the pictures from our great storehouses."

As the goblin said this a cloud rolled gradually away and disclosed a small and scantily furnished but neat apartment. Little children were gathered round a bright fire, clinging to their mother's gown, or gamboling round her chair. A frugal meal was spread upon the table and an elbow-chair was placed near the fire. Soon the father entered and the children ran to meet him. As he sat down to his meal the mother sat by his side and all seemed happiness and comfort. The meal was small and cheap: a tiny goose eked out by apple sauce, boiled potatoes, mashed in the saucepan, and gravy. It wasn't much of a Christmas dinner but it was sufficient for the whole family.

"What do you think of that?" said the goblin.

Gabriel murmured something about its being very pretty.

"Show him some more," said the goblin.

Many a time the cloud went and came, and many a lesson it taught Gabriel Grubb. He saw that men who worked hard and earned their scanty bread could be cheerful and happy. He saw that mothers and children with little enough to eat and drink could be joyful and glad. Even employers and their employees could be jovial and kind to one another. And he came to the conclusion that it could be a very respectable world after all; a world in which he, Gabriel Grubb, could be content, could be cheery, indeed perhaps could even be happy; that it was possible for him to make that choice.

No sooner had he formed this opinion than the cloud that closed over and the last picture seemed to settle on his senses and lull him to repose. One by one the goblins faded from his sight, and as the last one disappeared Gabriel sank into a deep sleep.

Christmas Day had broken when he awoke, and he found himself lying on the flat gravestone, with the wicker-bottle empty by his side. He was quite alone. There was no goblin nearby; he heard no voices crying, Gabriel Grubb, Gabriel Grubb.

He got to his feet as well as he could, and brushing the frost off his coat, turned his face towards the town and started to walk.

But he was an altered man, he had learned lessons of gentleness and good-nature by his strange adventure with the king of the goblins, by the visions he'd seen in the goblin's cavern.

And as he walked into the town, people heard a sound they'd never heard before. Gabriel Grubb could be heard to sing,

We wish you a Merry Christmas;

We wish you a Merry Christmas;

We wish you a Merry Christmas and a Happy New Year.

APPENDICES

Crackers: Christmas crackers are festive table decorations that make a snapping sound when pulled open, and often contain a small toy or trinket, a paper crown, and a joke, motto, riddle, or bit of trivia on a tiny strip of paper. They are part of Christmas celebrations in the UK, Ireland, and Commonwealth countries such as Australia (where they are sometimes known as bon bons), Canada, New Zealand, and South Africa. A cracker consists of a segmented cardboard tube wrapped in a brightly decorated twist of paper with a prize in the middle, making it resemble an over-sized sweet (candy) wrapper. The cracker is pulled apart by two people, each holding an outer chamber, causing the cracker to split unevenly and leaving one person holding the central chamber and prize. The split is accompanied by a mild bang or snapping sound produced by the effect of friction on a shock-sensitive, chemically impregnated card strip, similar to that used in a cap gun.

Crackers are typically pulled at the Christmas dinner table or at parties. In one version of the tradition, the person with the larger portion of cracker empties the contents from the tube and keeps them. In another, each person has their own cracker and keeps its contents regardless of whose end they were in. The paper hats, with the appearance of crowns, are usually worn when eating Christmas dinner. The tradition of wearing festive hats is believed to date back to Roman times and the Saturnalia celebrations, which also involved decorative headgear.

Adapted from Wikipedia

Pantomimes: The annual pantomime, customarily performed at Christmas with family audiences, is a popular form of theatre, incorporating song, dance, and other performance disciplines. It is a strictly British entertainment. Panto season sees productions in village halls and school auditoriums across the country, and it's hugely popular with amateur dramatic societies, or AMDRAMS. There is more detail on pantomimes later in the book.

St. Peter's School was later declared structurally unsafe and closed down. It was demolished and the site sold to Winchester City Council. It is now, alas, a carpark. Cue Joni Mitchell. . . .

Geordie: *Geordie* refers both to a native of Newcastle upon Tyne and to the speech of the inhabitants of that city. There are several theories about the exact origins of the term, but all agree it derives from the local pet name for George. It is sometimes mistakenly used to refer to the speech of the whole of the North East of England. Strictly speaking, however, Geordie should refer only to the speech of the city of Newcastle upon Tyne and the surrounding urban area of Tyneside.

Jonnie Robinson, Lead Curator for Spoken English at the British Library

Sisters of St. Lucy Filippini: Since first writing this account, I have discovered that Sister Mary belonged to the Congregation of the Religious Teachers Filippini, known also as the Sisters of St. Lucy Filippini, or simply the Filippini Sisters, a Catholic religious institute dedicated to education. They were founded in Italy in 1692 by Saint Lucy Filippini and Cardinal Marco Antonio Barbarigo. A group of sisters arrived in Winchester in June 1960, and at the invitation of Canon Mullarkey, started a convent and opened a nursery school.

From the History of St. Peter's Catholic Church

The widow's mite: Mark 12:41 "And Jesus sat over against the treasury, and beheld how the people cast money into the treasury:

and many that were rich cast in much. And there came a certain poor widow, and she threw in two mites, which make a farthing. And he called unto him his disciples, and saith unto them, 'Verily I say unto you, That this poor widow hath cast more in, than all they which have cast into the treasury: For all they did cast in of their abundance; but she of her want did cast in all that she had, even all her living.'"

From King James Bible

The Nigerian Civil War: The Biafran War (1967–1970) was fought over the formation of the state of Biafra, made up of states in Nigeria's Eastern Region, who declared their independence in May 1967. The conflict claimed the lives of as many as three million Biafran civilians who died of starvation, disease and injury.

From ChristianAid.org.uk

Council accommodation: Council houses and flats in the UK are the equivalent of public housing in the US.

Winchester Guildhall: Like much of the Roman City of Winchester, the Guildhall has a fascinating history. It stands on the site of an estate granted by King Alfred the Great to his wife, Ealhswith, probably as a coronation gift in AD 871. After his death she retired there and founded a nunnery, known as Nunnaminster. The nunnery was eventually dissolved by Henry VIII in 1539 and the land returned to the city's hands to help pay for hosting the wedding of Mary Tudor and Philip of Spain in Winchester Cathedral in 1554. The Victorian Gothic revival Guildhall, as it stands today, was built in 1871 and opened in May 1873 for civic purposes, also housing the law courts, police station, and fire brigade.

People in close proximity: I'm working on this book during the coronavirus (COVID-19) pandemic. Just writing the words "with all those bodies pressed together singing merrily" is causing my heart to beat a little faster!

Jebel Ali Hotel: In the 1980s, when I worked there, the Jebel Ali had a sister, the delightful Hatta Fort Hotel, which operates to this day, nestling in an oasis in the Hajjar mountains. According to my files, they traded under the name, Dutco Hotels, but I notice online, it says Jebel Ali International Hotels. Along with the rest of Dubai, the group has grown. The original, my place of work, is now called the Jebel Ali Beach Hotel and is part of a chain of hotels, known as JA The Resort. Until recently, that chain was called JA Jebel Ali Beach Hotel and Resort.

Jebel Ali Free Zone (Jafza): a free economic zone located in the Jebel Ali area at the far western end of Dubai, United Arab Emirates, between Dubai and Abu Dhabi. Created under a Ruler's Decree, Jafza commenced operations in 1985 with standard-size office units and warehouses to provide ready-built facilities to customers. In 1990 Jafza expanded its facilities to include light industrial units. It is the world's largest free zone.

The Palm Jebel Ali: an artificial archipelago in Dubai, United Arab Emirates, which began construction in October 2002. It was originally planned to be finished by mid-2008 and has been on hold since. While incomplete, this leaf-shaped island complex has a waterfront hotel with golf and a spa.

The Boss: As I began my Dubai stories (for my upcoming book, *Dinner in Dubai*), I became anxious about checking with people included in them. Unlike my life in Libya, I'm still in touch with friends and contacts from my time there and felt obliged to check that my memories even loosely matched theirs. One person whom this especially concerned was my boss at the Jebel Ali. I hoped not to offend or impact his life—he'd moved on by then and ran his own business—as not all my memories of him were positive ones. We'd stayed in touch during the rest of my years in Dubai, until I left in 1992. I'd also visited the Emirates on vacation in 1999 and he'd been proud to give me a full guided tour of the hotel, with all its additions and improvements. Years later, we became online friends, assisted by the advent of Facebook, and exchanged long chatty emails, and birthday, Christmas, and Ramadan greetings. He knew I was putting my overseas memories on paper and encouraged me. He was very supportive when it came to my first memoir, *Tea in Tripoli*. However, before I had a chance to run my Dubai drafts by him, he died in May 2019. It was a dreadful shock. I'd been worried about his opinions of my JAH stories, and now I was disappointed I wouldn't have him to verify them. More than that, though, I was genuinely saddened that I'd never hear that giggling laugh again, we'd never get to tease each other about what we might've seen as each other's "transgressions," and he'd never get to read this book sharing the dramatic and often hilarious moments of my eighteen months as his secretary and assistant. I'm still grieving.

Dinner in Dubai: Full stories about life in the Persian Gulf appear in my forthcoming memoir.

Monty Python's Australian wine sketch: "A lot of people in this country pooh-pooh Australian table wines. This is a pity, as many fine Australian wines appeal not only to the Australian palette, but also to the cognoscenti of Great Britain. 'Black stump Bordeaux' is rightly praised as a peppermint flavoured Burgundy, whilst a good 'Sydney Syrup' can rank with any of the world's best sugary wines. 'Chateau Bleu', too, has won many prizes; not least for its taste, and its lingering afterburn. 'Old Smokey, 1968' has been compared favourably to a Welsh claret, whilst the Australian wino society thoroughly recommends a 1970 'Coq du Rod Laver', which, believe me, has a kick on it like a mule: eight bottles of this, and you're really finished—at the opening of the Sydney Bridge Club, they were fishing them out of the main sewers every half an hour. Of the sparkling wines, the most famous is 'Perth Pink'. This is a bottle with a message in, and the message is BEWARE! This is not a wine for drinking—this is a wine for laying down and avoiding. Another good fighting wine is 'Melbourne Old-and-Yellow', which is particularly heavy, and should be used only for hand-to-hand combat. Quite the reverse is true of 'Chateau Chunder', which is an Appalachian controle, specially grown for those keen on regurgitation—a fine wine which really opens up the sluices at both ends. Real emetic fans will also go for a 'Hobart Muddy', and a prize winning 'Cuiver Reserve Chateau Bottled Nuit San Wogga Wogga', which has a bouquet like an aborigine's armpit."

From montypython.net

Gumby: a character generally played by Michael Palin, though the first was played by John Cleese. All of the Pythons have played one of them at one time or another. A Gumby is a character of limited intelligence and vocabulary. They speak haltingly, in a loud, indistinct manner.

Adapted from Wikipedia's List of Monty Python's Flying Circus Recurring Characters

Gary Glitter: Paul Francis Gadd (born 8 May 1944), known professionally as Gary Glitter, is an English glam rock singer who achieved success in the 1970s and 1980s, known for his extreme glam image of glitter suits, make-up, and platform boots, and his energetic live performances. He sold over 20 million records, had 26 hit singles that spent a total of 180 weeks in the UK Singles Chart, twelve reaching the Top 10, with three charting at number one. He is listed in the Top 100 UK most successful chart acts. He was imprisoned for downloading child pornography in 1999 and for child sexual abuse and attempted rape in 2006 and 2015. Formerly one of the best-loved entertainers in British music history, in 2015 Glitter was described by Alexis Petridis of *the Guardian* as a "public hate figure." His performances on the BBC's *Top of the Pops* are not repeated.

Adapted from Wikipedia

Aseef School: now the Dubai Centre for Special Needs.

St. Austin's Church: "St. Austin" is not a recognized saint. I used to think the church was named after the city. It is actually named for St. Augustine of Canterbury.

Keep Austin Weird: "Keep Austin Weird" is the slogan adopted by the Austin Independent Business Alliance to promote local businesses in Austin, Texas. It was inspired by comments made by Austin Community College librarian, Red Wassenich, in 2000 while giving a pledge to an Austin radio station. He operated www. keepaustinweird.com until his death in 2020. He published "Keep Austin Weird: A Guide to the Odd Side of Town."

Note about Editing: I was proud, when I finished editing *A Christmas Carol*, to end up with a similar script to the ones I'd performed in the past. I compared myself favorably with other theatre professionals and their editing ability. However, I was disappointed not to generate an alternative interpretation, a work I could call my own. I had wanted to reintroduce sections of the book that I hadn't seen on stage before, such as Scrooge's visits with the miners and lighthouse workers, but it wouldn't have been rational, due to time and technical limitations.

The Eight: Reindeer Monologues, book by Jeff Goode: "A wickedly funny alternative to traditional candy-cane cheer. Scandal erupts at the North Pole when one of Santa's eight tiny reindeer accuses him of sexual harassment. As the mass media descends upon the event, the other members of the sleigh team demand to share their perspectives, and a horrific tale of corruption and perversion emerges, which seems to implicate everyone from the teeniest elf to the tainted Saint himself. With each deer's stunning confession, the truth behind the shocking allegations becomes clearer . . . and murkier. Don't miss this hilarious holiday spectacle."
From the City Theatre's marketing, December 2011

The Blitz: In October 1940, Hitler ordered a massive bombing campaign against London and other cities to crush British morale and force an armistice. Despite significant loss of life and tremendous material damage to Britain's cities, the country's resolve remained unbroken. The ability of Londoners to maintain their composure had much to do with Britain's survival during this trying period. As

American journalist Edward R. Murrow reported, "Not once have I heard a man, woman, or child suggest that Britain should throw her hand." In May 1941, the air raids essentially ceased as German forces massed near the border of the USSR.

Adapted from History.com

Charles Dickens' "The Christmas Goblins": Francine entertains her guests during the bombing with Dickens' short story, "The Christmas Goblins," which is clearly the forerunner of his famous classic, *A Christmas Carol*.

Winchester German Market: Winchester Cathedral's Christmas Market is recognised as one of the best Christmas Markets in Europe because of its unique location, high-quality exhibitors and bustling atmosphere. Wonderful Christmas gifts, decorations and festive foods can be found in abundance, with a Food Court, British Crafts Village, and over 110 chalets to explore. In 2019, Winchester Cathedral Christmas Market was voted best Christmas market in the UK and one of the top 15 Christmas Markets in Europe by European Best Destinations. Traders travel from far and wide to participate. The Christmas Market is inspired by traditional German Christmas markets and attracts close to half a million visitors each year. The wooden chalets are situated in the Cathedral's historic Close surrounding an open-air real ice rink. All exhibitors have been hand-picked for their interesting, high quality and unique products.

From www.winchester-cathedral.org.uk

Premier Inn: Just a mile from the majesty of Winchester Cathedral town centre with its award-winning pubs, restaurants and a tempting array of independent shops, this hotel is ideally situated for business and leisure guests. This culturally-rich medieval city is surrounded by idyllic Hampshire villages and fabulous rolling countryside of the South Downs National Park. The hotel is within a half a mile of the M3 (J9), while the train station is just 1 mile away and has direct connections to London and the South. Winchester Hotel has everything you'd expect for a great stay, with 101 new generation bedrooms featuring impressive 40" flat screen TVs and brand new, slumber-inducing, king-size Hypnos beds, plus on-site Thyme restaurant and licensed bar.

From Trip Advisor

Highcliffe: Highcliffe-on-Sea (Highcliffe) is a small town in the borough of Christchurch, Dorset, in southern England. It forms part of the South East Dorset conurbation along the English Channel coast. The town lies on a picturesque stretch of Solent coastline with views of the Isle of Wight and its 'Needles' rocks. Highcliffe is situated to the east of the historic town of Christchurch and the resort town of Bournemouth, and to the west of Barton on Sea and New Milton. The New Forest National Park is to the north. Its position on the south coast gives it a climate with milder winters than inland areas, and less rainfall than locations further west. This helped establish the town as a popular health and leisure resort during the late Victorian and early Edwardian eras.

From Wikipedia

Lala's Little Nugget: Founded in 1972, Lala's Little Nugget has been one of the defining bars in Austin, Texas for decades. With the halls decked with boughs of holly year round, Santa and his reindeer perched on the roof and generations of Christmas memorabilia, Lala's is a North Pole oasis in Central Texas.

Adapted from www.lalasaustintexas.com